DAN JONES

Summer of Blood

The Peasants' Revolt of 1381

WILLIAM COLLINS

William Collins
An imprint of HarperCollins*Publishers*
1 London Bridge Street
London SE1 9GF

www.williamcollinsbooks.com

This William Collins paperback edition published 2014

First published in Great Britain by Harper*Press* in 2009

A catalogue record for this book is available from the British Library

ISBN 978-0-00-721393-1

Set in Minion by Palimpsest Book Production Limited
Grangemouth, Stirlingshire

Printed and bound in Great Britain by
CPI Group (UK) Ltd, Croydon CR0 4YY

MIX
Paper from
responsible sources
FSC **FSC™ C007454**
www.fsc.org

FSC is a non-profit international organisation established to promote the
responsible management of the world's forests. Products carrying the FSC
label are independently certified to assure consumers that they come
from forests that are managed to meet the social, economic
and ecological needs of present and future generations.

Find out more about HarperCollins and the environment at
www.harpercollins.co.uk/green

For my parents

CONTENTS

PART III

MAPS

Rebellious towns in Essex and Kent,
May and early June 1381

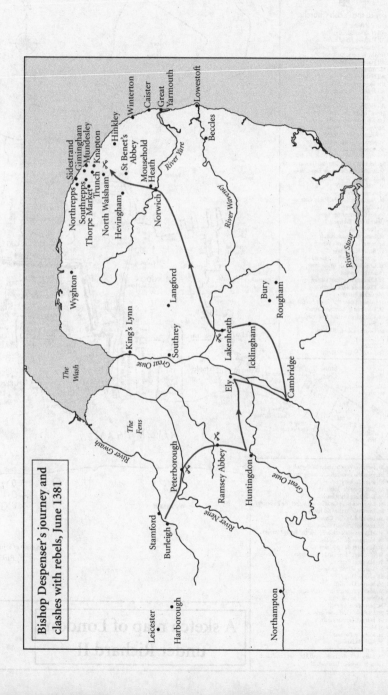

Bishop Despenser's journey and clashes with rebels, June 1381

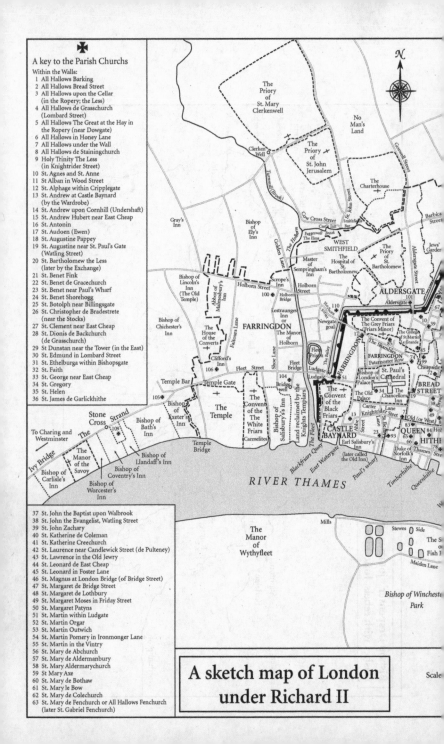

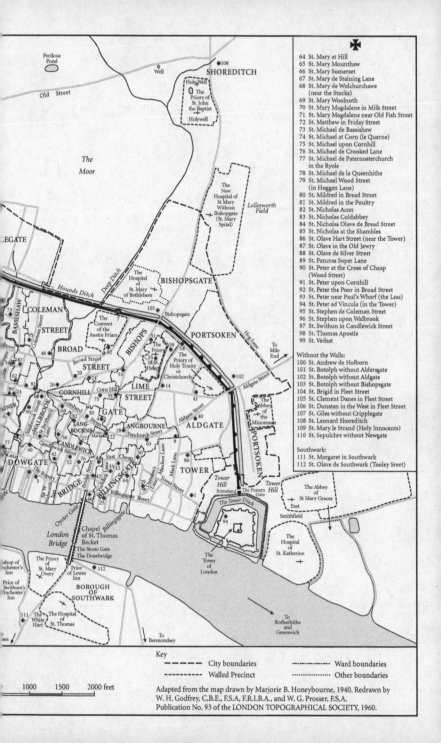

AUTHOR'S NOTE

Ten years ago I arrived at Pembroke College, Cambridge to read for the History Tripos. It was then – as much through random choice as good judgment – that I chose to study for the first time the history of medieval England.

It was hardly a fashionable choice. Medieval history was generally thought of as dirty, distant, a little alien or just quite boring At some faculty classes I was one of only five or six undergraduates in the whole university to be taking the subject. Lecture series about political thought, the Tudor household and Islamic history were packed, but the world-class lectures on crime and disorder in medieval England were sparsely populated. Cambridge had – and still has – some of the finest minds in the field, but few people were listening.

This struck me then, as now, as a great pity. But out in the real world, that trend continues. We know very well the business of the Tudors, the Victorians, the Romans and the Nazis. Yet we are broadly unfamiliar with events in Britain before 1485 – even though the Middle Ages not only established the character of our nation, but is also a rich seam of gripping stories.

I hope with this book, and the next one, to restore medieval history to the minds of readers all over the nation. I want to bring to life for a new generation the outrageous characters and episodes of heroism, villainy, glory and wickedness that were years ago ingrained in every school-leaver's mind. *Summer of Blood* is in that sense the start of a project. If you, the reader, enjoy this book, then I can be optimistic that it will be a successful one.

Now I must thank a number of people for this book's very existence. Kind and talented friends have made its writing not just possible, but hugely pleasurable. I thank them here with all the gratitude in my heart, and claim for myself total responsibility for any and all omissions, errors and plain old howlers.

In the first place, I must thank those brilliant teachers who have inspired me to read and write about history. Robin Green was the first. Later there were others: at Pembroke they included Jon Parry, the late Mark Kaplanoff and the late Clive Trebilcock. Then there were the medievalists: Christine Carpenter, Helen Castor and Richard Partington. Finally, David Starkey taught me much about writing and gave me faith in telling the stories of people and places rather than of abstract movements and the development of institutions.

I count myself among the happiest writers in London to have as my agent Georgina Capel. She has showed faith in me always, plucked me up from innumerable blue funks and given me the courage to write as I see true. She is extraordinary and brilliant.

My publisher, Arabella Pike, has been enthusiastic about this book from the beginning, and was very patient in waiting for it. She trusted me when I was but a stripling with a big idea, and I hope this book and the next will be some small reward for her belief. Her talented team at Harper Press also deserve much praise. In particular, I must thank Michael Upchurch for working with intelligence and understanding on the manuscript and Sophie Goulden for following my occasionally rather vague instructions to find the images and maps.

Leanda de Lisle was the first to suggest the possibility of writing about 1381, and has been an encouraging and constant friend and fellow historian throughout.

Paul Wilson and Walter Donahue were kind enough to read draft versions of various parts of the book and made very useful comments.

They are both hugely gifted and generous with their time – and I am proud and grateful to call them my friends.

The staff at the London Library, the British Library and Soho House brought me books, maps and wine, all of which were vital.

Finally, my fiancée, Jo Scotchmer, has been with me throughout. She tolerated me reading chapters aloud before bedtime, and managed my occasional despair with cheerful good grace. She is my true friend and my foundation.

Thanks and love to all.

DJ

They're both listening still . . . and spoken with their fans – and I am proud and grateful to call them my friends.

The staff at the London Library, the parish Library, and Toms House brought me books, maps and . . . all of which were . . . cially invaluable. In so doing, . . . has been with me throughout . . . She ushered me reading through . . . words before bedtime and managed my occasional despair with cheerful good grace. She is my . . . ride behind and my foundation.

Anyhow. Love to all.

FOREWORD

'A revell! A revell!'[1]

No one could forget the noise when Wat Tyler led his ragtag army of roofers and farmers, bakers, millers, ale-tasters and parish priests into the City of London on a crusade of bloodthirsty justice. It filled the City for days: frantic screaming and cries of agony that accompanied acts of butchery and chaos. It was as if, thought one observer, all the devils in hell had found some dark portal and flooded into the City.[2]

Tyler's army screamed on Corpus Christi, the morning on which they stormed over London Bridge and swarmed from the streets of Southwark, leaving smouldering brothels and broken houses behind them as they headed for the streets of the capital. They howled with demented joy when they sacked and burned down the Savoy – one of the greatest palaces in Europe and the pride of England's most powerful nobleman. They screeched like peacocks when they dragged royal councillors from the Tower and beheaded them, and again when they joined native Londoners in pulling terrified Flemish merchants from their sanctuary inside churches and hacking them to death in the streets.

The great rebellion of summer 1381, driven by the mysterious general Wat Tyler and the visionary northern preacher John Ball, was one of the most astonishing events of the later Middle Ages. A flash rising of England's humblest men and women against their

1

richest and most powerful countrymen, it was organised in its early stages with military precision and ended in chaos.

Between May and August rebellion swept through virtually the entire country. It was sparked by a series of three poll taxes, each more recklessly imposed than the last, and all played out against a background of oppressive labour laws that had been imposed to keep the rich rich and the poor poor. But more broadly the rebellion was aimed at what many ordinary people in England saw as a long and worsening period of corrupt, incompetent government and a grievous lack of social justice. Like most rebellions, it was the sum of many murky parts. There was a radical cabal at the centre proposing a total overhaul of the organisation of English government and lordship. Their zeal swept along thousands of honest but discontented working folk who agreed with the general sentiment that things, in general, ought to be better. And at the fringes there were many opportunistic plunderers, disgruntled score-settlers and the incorrigibly criminal, to whom any opportunity for violence and theft was welcome.[3]

The rebellion's focal point and moment of high drama came in London on the festival weekend of Thursday 13 to Sunday, 16 June. On that weekend a crowd of thousands, who had marched to London from the Kentish capital of Canterbury on a sort of anti-pilgrimage, joined with an excited mob drawn from the common people of the capital to demonstrate, riot and pass judgement on their rulers. They came within a whisker of taking down the entire royal government. London, which had been riven with faction and anti-government sentiment for nearly five years, collapsed into anarchy within hours of the rebels' arrival on the south bank of the River Thames. Finding no shortage of allies within its walls, the rebels achieved in an astonishingly short time the total paralysis of government, the terrorisation of the most important men in the state and the destruction of the Savoy Palace and many other beautiful buildings. Public order dissolved, and was restored only at the highest cost to the Crown. And after a period of what amounted to military rule across London, the country remained at risk of terror from within for months, first fearing a repeat of the rebellion, and subsequently brutalised by a judicial counter-terror that lasted for most of the rest of the year. It would change the course of English history for ever.

Outside London, the rebellious spirit proved infectious, and there were major revolts in Essex, Kent and East Anglia, as well as more isolated riots and urban disorder in Somerset, Sussex, Oxfordshire, Leicestershire and Yorkshire. Even once the troubled summer had faded into autumn, plotting continued throughout England, and the subject of lower-order resistance, present in literature from the middle of the fourteenth century, became a real concern for the well-to-do.

In short, the rebellion was both a comprehensive damnation of English government and a startling announcement of the new political consciousness of the common folk of England. The lower orders, who had for generations been treated by the landed and powerful as little more than beasts of burden and battlefield fodder, showed themselves to be dangerous, politically aware, and capable both of independent military organisation and blistering anger. England's nobility, merchants, lawyers and wealthy churchmen – most of whom had long suspected in the labouring class a tendency to viciousness – were confirmed in all their worst fears. The revolt marked the beginning of a rebellious tradition among the English lower orders which has been repeated ever since – from Jack Cade's rebels in 1450 to Robert Ket's in 1549; from Lord Gordon's riots in 1780 to the famous 'poll tax' rebellion of our own time, in the early spring of 1990.

Over the centuries, the Peasants' Revolt – to use the slightly misleading shorthand that historians have given the rebellion – has found its place in the corpus of great events in English history. The year 1381 is a signpost on the road from the battle of Hastings in 1066 and Magna Carta in 1215 to Bosworth in 1485, the Armada in 1588 and everything beyond.

But what do we really know about it?

The truth is that, as with many historical phenomena, telling the whole story of the revolt can be like trying to nail a jelly to the wall. The sources are fragmentary, incomplete and strongly slanted in favour of the rebels' victims. The revolt's causes – economic, social, political and legal – were myriad, and its geographical spread was wide. The terror that was struck into the hearts of those who recorded the revolt has lingered on. England's monastic chroniclers recorded the rebels' crimes and England's lawyers documented their punishments. All did so with extreme prejudice, smearing the memories of the hated peasants with the ordure of their disgust, and staining the historical memory of the revolt with class hatred. Partly as a consequence, this class dimension has, over the years, attracted historians with a greater interest in applying historical theory than in fulfilling the historian's most important duty: to tell, as accurately as possible, a cracking good story.[4]

This book is an attempt to redress the balance: to bring back to life one of the most colourful episodes in our history. In 1381 the peasants burst onto the historical record, and they left, for all the prejudice of their victim-biographers, a wealth of vivid, violent, hysterical and occasionally hilarious reactions to posterity. Their story is a frenzied, bloodied trip into an under-explored period of English history. And its inevitable, gory conclusion – both tragic and reassuring – is a reminder of the cold truth of revolt: that even the most righteous rebels usually end up with their heads on spikes.

In writing this new narrative of the revolt, I have aimed to make the causes succinct, the action as vivid as it was then, and the consequences and vengeance wreaked by a humiliated government as terrible as they seemed to a chastened people. The result, I hope, is a journey into a world both profoundly different and remarkably similar to our own. The Peasants' Revolt takes us somewhere dimly lit and obscure: a world that could be unfair and outrageous; where death, pain, disease, discomfort and misery formed the fabric of everyday life for all but the very rich; a world where a large chunk of the population lived in some form of legal bondage to the land; a world of severe discipline and ingrained violence; a world where a man's last vision might be his own intestines burning in a pile on the ground.

But this was also a world of life, colour and touching humanity, where ambition could take a man from serfdom to prosperity; where charity and social responsibility, as much as chastisement and rebuke, bound lords and their lessers; and where, among the filth, poverty and violence, there was a belief in the potential to make things better.

Clearly, this was also a superstitious, deeply hierarchical world, often idiotically governed and ripe with casual brutality. But working on the drafts of this in London between 2007 and 2009, it was occasionally surprising how close it felt!

Dan Jones
London, 2009

INTRODUCTION

In 1390 John Gower, the famous Kentish landowner and poet, reflected at great and gloomy length on the state of the world he saw around him. He was writing a cheerless book called *Vox Clamantis* ('The Voice of One Crying Out'), in which he described how man grew increasingly feckless, corrupt and base, turning from God, obsessed by material gain, and ripe for divine punishment.

Nowhere, thought Gower, was the iniquity of the world and the wrath of the Almighty quite so obvious as in the events of June 1381, when the flocks of rural yokels – many of them from his own county – had descended on London, torching houses, slaughtering their social superiors, and terrifying the life out of anyone who got in their way.

'Behold,' he wrote, remembering London that summer, 'it was Thursday, the Festival of Corpus Christi, when madness hemmed in every side of the city.

> Going ahead of the others, one captain urged them all to follow him. Supported by his many men, he crushed the city, put the citizens to the sword, and burned down the houses. He did not sing out alone, but drew many thousands along with him, and involved them in his nefarious doings. His voice gathered the madmen together, and with a cruel eagerness for slaughter he shouted in the ears of the rabble, 'Burn! Kill!'

The captain was Wat Tyler. He was leading a shabby but well-organised army in an attack on the private palace of the figurehead of government and the man whom the English populus blamed for everything that had gone awry in recent years – John of Gaunt, duke of Lancaster.

'What had been the Savoy burned fiercely in the flames, so that Lancaster did not know which path to take,' Gower wrote. He then turned to Tyler's other crimes against London's ancient buildings. 'The Baptist's house, bereft of its master, fell to the sword and was soon ashes because of the flames. Holy buildings burned in wicked fires, and shameless flame was thus mixed with a sacred flame. The astonished priests wept with trembling heart and fear took away their body's strength.'

Gower was a man given to melancholy. In that, he was a man of his time. He had grown up in a world of sufficient hardship to turn any man to apocalyptic woe. When Gower was seven, England had gone to war with France, sparking a conflict that would put Kent and the rest of the south coast in perpetual danger of looting and raiding. When he was eighteen, the first wave of a vicious plague that wiped out between 40 and 50 per cent of the English population swept across the country, returning in epidemic after epidemic throughout Gower's middle years. When he was fifty-two, Tyler's mob had wrought carnage upon towns, cities and manor houses from Canterbury to York. And the very next year an earthquake had shaken the country, in many places quite literally to its foundations.

But of all this misery, it was the revolt of 1381 which made the most profound impression on Gower. He saw it with his own eyes, and thought it symbolic of the madness, faithlessness and viciousness of man, which had angered God so much that he sent down acts of destruction worthy of the Old Testament.

With the exception of Chaucer, who remembered the brutal massacre of 140 Flemish merchants by an assorted mob of Londoners and invaders from the shires in rather breezy terms ('He Jakke Straw, and his meynee/Ne made never shoutes half so shrille/Whan that they wolden any Flemyng kille'[1]), Gower's reaction broadly represented the appalled majority of England's rich and powerful. The revolt was pregnant with significance – in the eyes of contemporaries it became, variously, a sign from God, the work of Satan, a fit of lunacy, a monkish plot, a heretic crusade, a city siege and, in the words of the French chronicler Jean Froissart, 'a rustic tragedy'.

Rooting through the archives of Cambridge's University Library in 1895, the celebrated Victorian historian G. C. Macaulay discovered a hitherto unknown work by John Gower. It was called the *Mirour de l'omme*, and had been written around 1378. Though no less glum than *Vox Clamantis*, it had been written before the revolt, rather than after it. In that sense, it added a new dimension to Gower's pious condemnation of Tyler's rebellion. In it, the poet actually seemed to have predicted a popular uprising.

In his eyes, the 1370s had been taut with expectation of a catastrophic failure of the social order – one in which the angry mob would break its shackles and turn on the powerful men of England with terrible force. England's neighbour, France, had already seen such a revolt, in the Jacquerie of 1358, when the common people in the Oise valley, north of Paris, had risen up against their lords, in protest against punitive taxation and the inept conduct of the war with England. In the *Mirour*, Gower wrote:

> There are three things of such a sort,
> that they produce merciless destruction
> when they get the upper hand.
> One is a flood of water,
> another is a raging fire
> and the third is the lesser people,
> the common multitude;
> for they will not be stopped
> by either reason or discipline.

Gower, Chaucer and their contemporaries referred to the 'lesser people' in a number of different ways. The monastic chroniclers, writing in Latin, usually called them *rustica* and *villani*, from which English translations over the years have given us 'yokel', 'rustic', 'serf', 'villein', 'churl', 'bondsman' and, of course, 'peasant'. There are two common connotations: these people were uneducated rural folk, and (especially in the case of serf, villein, churl and bondsman) they were to some extent 'tied' to the land via ancient, hereditary, personal obligations to their landlords.

Though the rising is commonly called the Peasants' Revolt, it is that translation which causes most problems. The word 'peasant' has become so commonplace over the years that it is now all but cliché. It is all too easy in thinking about the peasants to fall back on the vision of dirty, ill-educated farmhands in sackcloth, leading short, identical lives of brutal frugality.

The truth is more complicated. By the late fourteenth century the English economy had grown very diverse, and particularly in the south-east there was a flourishing market economy. The ordinary people of England were not simply self-sustaining tenant farmers – they had jobs, trades and specialities. The laws concerning England's labourers referred to carters and ploughmen, shepherds and swineherds, domestic servants, carpenters, masons, roofers, thatchers, shoemakers, goldsmiths, horse-smiths, spurriers, tanners, plasterers and 'those who provide carriage by land or water'. England was not yet a nation of shopkeepers but it was a diverse and sophisticated nation nonetheless, with an economy that joined communities to one another and the country to the markets of continental Europe.

The everyday folk in England's rural communities lived in villages – straggling clutches of two-roomed thatched houses populated by small families of three or four people. They were not quite the dense, nucleated villages we know today, but they were organised settlements all the same and they had social structures and mores to govern life. Village houses were usually set along a main road, in the middle of which stood a church, perhaps a village green, where animals were grazed, and the village manor. Around the village would be three or four large fields – sprawling acres of unfenced land divided into strips.

Each family rented a strip from the local lord, who would also have a large portion of the land set aside for himself.

Between the time of the Norman Conquest in 1066 and the end of the fourteenth century, large numbers of the common people of England paid their rent for the small plots of land that fed them in the form of compulsory, hereditary labour service for a lord. Systems of tenure and the jurisdictions of lords varied across the country and did not always fit neatly and discretely with the organisation of the village, but lordship existed everywhere. As a rough rule, the lord would demand a certain number of days' free or compulsory paid labour from his tenants every year. Froissart described the peasants' typical duties: they were 'bound by law and custom to plough the field of their masters, harvest the corn, gather it into barns, and thresh and winnow the grain; they must also mow and carry home the hay, cut and collect wood, and perform all manner of tasks of this kind'. In reality, there was more to it than this, but the principle of labouring for one's lord endured. There was little freedom to swap lords and in many areas serfdom (the total ownership of a servant by his or her master) still ran strong. A runaway serf, if caught, would have his back whipped, or his ears cropped, or his face branded.

By the fourteenth century, however, a great number of serfs had been set free, and their labour dues had been combined with or replaced by cash rents. Villages might contain a mixture of serfs and freemen, and there were degrees of hierarchy within the village, well below the level of the lord. Many whose ancestors had been serfs had managed to wriggle out of the bonds of tenure, acquired free legal status and started to speculate in land, employing other men and women from their villages, protecting their property in law and adopting the mindset of the upwardly mobile.

But for all, the bond of lordship remained strong. Whether land was rented, owned or occupied in return for forced labour, lordship was a two-way relationship and the great landowners of England wielded considerable political and legal power over the lesser. The lord, sitting as judge in his manor court, ultimately protected the property of his tenants, which affected everyone in the area. Should a village man find himself in a dispute; should his son be crippled or his daughter kidnapped; should his home be burned or his land stolen; should he wake up to find his sheep's throats slit, or their wool shorn and ghosted away in the night, it was usually to his lord he turned for restitution, protection or judgement.

There were, of course, disadvantages. Some lords had a nasty habit of screwing every last advantage out of their position and could insist on claiming various irritating slices of often meagre peasant incomes, such as a sweetener when a daughter married, or a fee on inheriting a father's property. Villagers were expected to turn out as the rent-a-mob when the lord required muscle in disputes with his neighbours. (They were largely untrained in the martial arts – although skill with a longbow was a hallmark of the English army in the fourteenth century, only the knightly classes had the spare time and money to become truly dangerous. When called to battle, the lower orders mainly provided crossbow fodder.) And they might be called upon to defend the realm itself. For some this meant battle on the Continent; for others, especially villagers on the south coast, the fourteenth century was one of intermittent defence against burning and looting by French raiding parties.

Yet despite the occasional irritations, and the intrusions of life's grimmer realities, the various strata of English society had lived in relatively peaceful coexistence since at least the days of the Conquest. Medieval life was acutely hierarchical, with a sense of place in the world inseparable from ideas of Christian duty and the belief in a divinely ordained order of the universe. Charity and paternalism on the lords' side was largely reciprocated by deference and respect for authority on their tenants'. Villages could not be policed in the sense that we would understand it now, and a sensitive lord understood that he had to work his estate management and local government through the existing village hierarchies. More senior men in the village were needed to perform administrative tasks for the lord, and to broker potentially unpopular lordly demands with the lesser men of their communities.

The two-way relationship was reinforced by the ample scope that existed for rising up through the ranks. The path out of drudgery and toil was well trodden. William Wykeham, bishop of Winchester from 1367 to 1371, was probably the son of a peasant. Clement Paston, a plough-pushing fourteenth-century churl, founded the letter-writing Pastons of Norfolk, one of the fifteenth century's best-known gentry dynasties. If the relationship was managed correctly, there did not need to be perpetual strife between lords and tenants, and for the most part, there was not.

In 1381, though, there was a violent and total rejection of lordship. Hostility to the ancient social structures produced the 'merciless destruction' prophesied by Gower. The common multitude rose, and yielded, just as predicted, to neither reason nor discipline. Why?

The answer is complex, and the only way to unravel the rage of the rebels in 1381 is to delve deep into a society that had been creaking into an unfamiliar shape during the previous thirty years. There was no single event to blame for the revolt but several burned fiercely underneath. The most important was the arrival of the most ruthless killer England had seen then, or has seen since: the Black Death.

The Black Death arrived from continental Europe, probably via the Channel Islands, in the summer of 1348. Bristol, Southampton and Melcombe Regis (now Weymouth) suffered first, and from the ports the plague spread at a rate of between one and five miles a day, wiping out almost half of the English population. Sufferers succumbed to one of three equally nasty variations: the bubonic plague, in which buboes or tumours as big as eggs or even apples would appear on the neck, armpits and groin, bringing death within a week; a second variation, spread by the breath, attacked the respiratory system, and usually killed its victims within forty-eight hours. A septicaemic version also appeared, attacking the blood system, which led to internal haemorrhaging, causing dark blotches grimly referred to as 'God's tokens' all over the body.

As people across Europe began to sicken and die, the Italian writer Giovanni Boccaccio called the Italian epidemic a sign of God's wrath.

The Scots, meanwhile, rashly adjudged it a sign of God's specific wrath at the English and 'were accustomed to swear "be the foul deth of Engelond"'.[2]

But the plague made no distinction between Scots and English, and it had little respect for social hierarchy. Nobles and gentry across Europe tried their best to avoid the plague by shutting themselves away in their houses, but the plague was too virulent. Remedies prescribed included posies of flowers held by the nose, drinking and debauchery in taverns, isolation at home, bleeding and prayer. None worked, and though the richest in society could afford to sample the more extravagant medicines (King Edward III, suffering from dysentery, was once prescribed an electuary of ambergris, musk, pearls, gold and silver, which cost £134, or around three knights' yearly incomes combined) they did not escape untouched. Archbishops died in the same agonies as their subordinates and dioceseans: in July 1349 the Pope consecrated the new archbishop of Canterbury, Thomas Bradwardine, in Rome. He died of the plague within two days of his return to England. The common people of England died in such great quantities that their bodies were often simply piled into trenches by the willing few who could be found to dispose of them. An accompanying plague among oxen and sheep left the countryside littered with carcasses 'rotted so much that neither bird nor beast would touch them'.[3]

The grim mortality caused great alarm across Europe, but in England the economic effects of the plague worried the government just as much. In 1349 Edward III rushed out a royal command – the Ordinance of Labourers. 'Because a great part of the people, and especially of workmen and servants, late[ly] died of the pestilence,' read the proclamation, 'many seeing the necessity of masters, and great scarcity of servants, will not serve unless they may receive excessive wages.' In other words plague survivors could suddenly become rich. Having scrabbled for work in an employers' market before the Black Death, the English lower orders could suddenly name their price. This was very worrying. The official response – ratified in the 1351 parliament as the Statute of Labourers – was to set up a rigorous system of wage and price fixing, setting out maximum daily rates of pay for almost every profession imaginable. Farmers, saddlers, tailors, fishmongers, butchers, brewers, bakers and every other labourer and artisan in England were prevented from charging more than pre-plague prices for their goods or work; and they were committing a crime if they did not 'serve him which shall so require' – meaning they had to work wherever and whenever they were instructed. Punishments were tough – three days' imprisonment in the stocks for first offenders, fines (300 per cent of the offending mark-up for shopkeepers who hiked their prices) and imprisonment for the obstinate.

From the day it was published, the Statute of Labourers was greeted with a mixture of hostility, contempt and point-blank refusal. Even in an age devoid of economic theory, the sheer injustice of tampering with natural supply and demand was obvious. So was its futility. As demand for workers raced well ahead of supply, the law quickly became unworkable. But that did not stop landowners trying to enforce it. Wage demands rose and rents crashed in the absence of tenants to fill the land, and the greater landlords found the basis of their fortunes crumbling. Prosecutions under the new labour laws rocketed. By the 1370s, 70 per cent of legal business in the king's courts involved the labour legislation, and this – along with lords' newly enthusiastic use of their own private manor courts to force workers to perform as much labour service as possible – quickly sowed a culture of discontent and resistance to the law among the lower orders.[4] Far from protecting them, the royal law was being used to harass them, to question their right to earn their worth, and to prevent them from acquiring and protecting their property.

From the position of the aristocracy, however, the labour laws made good sense. The sudden affluence of the rough-and-tumble village folk was threatening the divine and visible order of society just as much as the state of their private wealth. Rather than a fair rise in the value of labour, they saw what the Statute of Labourers called 'the malice of servants who were idle and unwilling to serve after the pestilence without taking outrageous wages'.[5] They began to see ambitious and wealthy villagers adopting habits above their station, dressing smartly and affecting the appearance of their betters. Gower, writing in characteristic animal allegory, described how 'the asses now took it upon themselves to enjoy jewelled saddles and always have their manes combed'. So in 1363 Parliament approved a reissue of the twenty-five-year-old sumptuary laws to attempt to preserve a visible distinction between the classes. The laws restricted the wearing of furs, or the increasingly popular pointed shoes, to nobles (who were allowed toe extensions of up to 24 inches), gentlemen (12 inches) and merchants (6.5 inches). They also forbade the lower orders to eat anything but the most basic foodstuffs.

For the workers, suddenly feeling the full weight of royal law, the legislation was a gross affront. It attacked not just the wages in their pocket but their dreams of betterment. Society had loosened its strictures on social advancement during previous generations – now all that was under threat, and the spectre of a new serfdom loomed over villages across the English countryside. It was not, perhaps, the old manorial system, but the laws seemed gradually to be reinstating the misery of bondage by any other name.

All this tension, then, was growing worryingly obvious as the 1370s advanced. It did not need a visionary like Gower to see it. Soon the commons in Parliament (which mainly represented and contained members of the gentry) began to complain of greater and greater hostility from the lower orders, who 'have made confederation and alliance together to resist the lords and their officials by force . . . and they threaten to kill their lords' servants if they make distraint upon them for their customs and services'.[6] All across the country there was resistance. There was a real sense that the English lower orders were gaining a sense of their own independent power. As a threat to society and the godly composition of the realm, this was very worrying. In the medieval world-view, consistent relations between the estates of society was a founding principle of Christian order.

And yet powerful economic forces prevailed. Egged on by unscrupulous itinerant lawyers, villagers all over the country were known to be making attempts to secure free status in the royal courts.

Whole villages began to claim special status under the terms of the Domesday Book, arguing that this ancient document proved their freedom from all number of lordly claims on their labour and wealth. The autumn of 1376 had given birth to the 'Great Rumour', a movement that had taken place across the fertile heartland of the south. Villagers started employing lawyers and instructing them to apply for "exemplifications" of Domesday.[7] (These were certified copies of the section of the Book that reported on the state of the village at the time of the Norman Conquest; copies that were presented neatly with an impression of the Great Seal of Chancery on the front.)

Between 1376 and 1377, nearly 100 villages asked for copies of Domesday. Getting hold of an exemplification was not the most opaque legal process of all, but it demanded legal savvy, ready cash and good contacts with the legal system in London. That ordinary villagers were suddenly rich, smart and bold enough to engage with law and politics made landowners very uneasy indeed. And when legal machinations were combined in some cases with outright threats to kill and maim their enemies, England's governing class began to worry that it would not be long before the threats became reality.

Added to this thick soup of social discord was the constant threat of war. From 1336, early in Edward III's reign, England had been engaged in a bitter, bloody struggle with France. Historians have called it the Hundred Years War, although in truth it was fought intermittently for 116 years. In the beginning, with Edward III a young man, a competent general and a forceful political negotiator, the war went well. England claimed glorious victories at sea and on land, owing mainly to the English mastery of the longbow – which could send an arrow through French armour, and could kill a horse with little difficulty from long range. War focused the realm and charmed the nobility, and Edward III, with a keen eye for internal diplomacy, made the overriding object of his reign one thing, and one thing alone: to capture the French throne.

To any English king in any century, conquering France was a grand ambition. Not only was the French kingdom territorially larger than the English, it was also much more difficult to maintain an army separated by the Channel. It had to be supplied at least in part from home soil and any successfully annexed territory had to be defended by expensive garrisons. The costs could be onerous.

But if the costs were high, the prize was deeply alluring. To place England at the heart of European intrigue brought glory to the English Crown. It gave the native English aristocracy, who led the wars and embraced the culture of chivalry, a profound sense of martial purpose, while the rank-and-file recruits were always happy to visit France, where the chance of decent plunder was higher than when raiding the freezing border towns in southern Scotland.

In partnership with his son Prince Edward (known to historians as the Black Prince), the young Edward III claimed resounding victories across France. At the battle of Crécy in 1346, the king thrust the sixteen-year-old prince into the centre of a stunning victory over superior French forces; he emerged victorious, the French utterly defeated and many of their own nobility dead on the battlefield.

The successes piled up. Later in 1346 the Scottish king David II had been captured near Durham and the next year, back in France, the English had conquered Calais, providing them with a French port that would remain English for two centuries. But the high point came at Poitiers in 1356, when an army led by Prince Edward was stalking through south-west France and came upon the French army led by King Jean. Battle was given and the prince, using similar archer-led tactics to those deployed at Crécy, routed the French army, slew a great many of the French nobles and seized the French king.

The result of this victory was the Treaty of Bretigny, signed and ratified in 1360/61, in which Edward III laid claim to great swathes of French territory. This included Gascony, several counties in northern France and the area around Calais. King Jean was ransomed at massive cost, and the prestige of the English Crown was raised to truly incredible heights. Bretigny was the high point of Edwardian kingship. In many ways, it was the high point of the English fourteenth century, a time when France was the enemy, England the mighty victor and kingship at home was proud and strong.

But momentum was required, and after Bretigny, English fortunes began to wane. In 1364 the captive King Jean, still under ransom, died in London, and his successor, Charles V, proved an astute political rival to Edward, frustrating his ambitions in Flanders and Brittany, resisting his efforts to cement English influence in France and allying with the Castilians to oppose Prince Edward's rule in Gascony. As Edward's reign wore on, the glorious victories began to dry up, and the considerable expense of paying for an army in the field became an increasing burden on a country that simply could not cope with the demands of a protracted war footing. The Black Prince contracted dysentery on campaign in Castile and suffered a lingering, painful death. At the same time, Edward himself grew increasingly feeble and senile, until by the 1370s his rule and his royal servants were under constant attack from the taxpaying classes, who were heartily sick of pumping cash into the yawning maw of a war bogged down in its own ambition. The dream, so nearly achieved and painstakingly won, was beginning to slip by.

In the parliament of 1376, with Edward close to death and the Black Prince fresh in his grave, the political community went on the attack. The focus was in the parliamentary commons, which comprised the upper middling ranks of English society – knights, town burgesses, large landholders and influential county men. They liked to complain of having been squeezed tightest by the war. Taxation hit them proportionally harder than the upper ranks of the nobility, while the costs of managing their estates had rocketed after the Black Death. They complained bitterly that they were 'seriously distressed in several ways by several misfortunes such as the wars in France, Spain, Ireland, Guienne, Brittany and elsewhere',[8] and began to demand political reform.

The result was the Good Parliament, as shocking an expression of general political discontent as had been seen for more than thirty years. The king's household was purged and his mistress, Alice Perrers, was severely castigated. The process of impeachment was used for the first time, aimed against royal servants who were widely blamed for the mismanagement of the war chest and the corruptions of the court. Richard Lyons, who was chief among the super-wealthy London merchants who partially bankrolled the war by loans to the Crown, and won royal favour in return, was impeached and imprisoned, as were several other key figures of the commons' ire. This was a stark repudiation of royal government, which even the eulogies that attended the deaths of the Black Prince and Edward III, in 1376 and 1377 respectively, could not disguise.

Neither did the future seem very promising. When the king died, the throne passed to the Black Prince's son, Richard of Bordeaux, a nine-year-old boy who had grown up knowing nothing of the glory of his grandfather's and father's achievements, but only their final years of weakness and decay. Around Richard was left the rump of the royal family, led by his uncles Thomas of Woodstock, the young earl of Buckingham, Edmund Langley, the earl of Cambridge, and John of Gaunt, the duke of Lancaster.

During his father's and elder brother's decline, Gaunt had leadership of government, and this thankless task had earned him few friends. He was an abrasive man and a second-rate military leader. From 1377 Gaunt did his best to hold the war effort together, but in France nothing short of a destructive stalemate seemed possible. At this point morale in the south-east was lower than at any time in the past century. Desertions from the underpaid army were rife; the towns on the south coast were full of men who had abandoned the hapless war effort. Furthermore, England's enemies were becoming increasingly bold in their attacks on the English coast, and raiding parties of French and Spanish pirates cruised up and down the Channel, disembarking to terrorise, burn and pillage the English. Londoners were so worried that plans were under way to erect a giant chain gateway across the Thames to prevent raiding parties from burning the city. The threat of invasion, which had not been a realistic possibility since the dark days at the end of King John's reign in 1216, suddenly loomed.

Heartily sick of paying regular and heavy taxation to a government they considered totally incompetent, the commons hatched a plan. Instead of bearing the brunt of the cost of defending the realm themselves, at the last parliament of Edward III's reign, held in Westminster in January and February 1377, they proposed a poll tax. Four pence was to be taken from every man and woman over the age of fourteen. This was a huge shock: taxation had never before been universal, and four pence was the equivalent of three days' labour to simple farmhands at the rates set in the Statute of Labourers. But to the commons it seemed perfectly logical. They had watched the lower orders enriching themselves with outrageous wage demands since the late 1340s – here was an excellent way of checking that worrying trend while defending the realm at the same time. The tax was passed.

Within four months of Parliament granting the poll tax, Edward III was dead. But there was no sign that the reign of his nine-year-old grandson was going to be anything less than turbulent. When Richard II was crowned in July 1377, the realm was already badly shaken. The first poll tax – met with widespread popular disgruntlement – was quickly swallowed up by the war effort. The government remained virtually bankrupt, reliant on massive loans from the City of London and pawning royal treasure to stay afloat. Peace negotiations with the French had collapsed in June, and by August the south coast was under attack. English military tactics were unsophisticated, based around the *chevauchée* – a rather glamorous term for what was essentially a travelling riot of looting, burning, rape and murder. Meanwhile, Frenchmen 'looted and set fire to several places' and took 1000 marks in ransom for the Isle of Wight. 'Then they returned to the sea and sailed along the English coastline continuously until Michaelmas [29 September]. They burned many places and killed, especially in the southern areas, all the people they could find . . . They carried off animals and other goods as well as several prisoners.'9

The first two parliaments of Richard's reign were noisy with complaint. Government ministers made frenzied attempts to wheedle money from the commons in any way they could. They were largely unsuccessful. With every fiscal failure, the threat of invasion grew more acute. By the spring of 1379 it had reached the point of crisis. Inspired perhaps by desperation, a radical new form of poll tax was agreed. Instead of a flat fee, a carefully graduated scale of payments according to class was developed. Earls were to pay £4, 'each baron and banneret or knight who is able to spend as much as a baron' was to pay 40s, judges and the richest lawyers were to pay 100s (£5). Laymen, once again, were to pay four pence, but there were fifty categories and a further eighteen subcategories of assessment. It was in essence a much fairer tax than the crude flat levy of 1377. But it was not enough.

Eight months after the second poll tax had been granted, Parliament was recalled. The government had expected to raise a bare minimum of £50,000. But £50,000 was the very least that could sustain the army, with its substantial mercenary element, on the rampage for a whole year. Yet following widespread evasion of the second poll tax, the proceeds amounted to less than £22,000. Abandoning the project, the parliament of January 1380 agreed a heavy tax on movable goods. That, too, was completely inadequate and the funds were immediately swallowed up by the duke of Buckingham's *chevauchée* through northern France.

Reality began to bite: the country was broke; the king, at thirteen years old, was too young to fix it; Gaunt, governing as regent-elect, was considered by the general population and especially by the money-men of London to be an arrogant, bungling swine; there was acute tension in the countryside and rumours of plans for widespread violence; the south coast was burning; the French garrisons were mutinous; the armies were deserting; the Scots were fomenting plans to invade; and things were only going to get worse. Either a radical solution was required or, at the very least, a huge amount of cash was needed to save the Crown from calamity.

So, in November 1380, yet another parliament was called.

PART I

PART 1

ONE

PARLIAMENT

The lords and commons are agreed that to meet the necessities above
mentioned three groats should be given from each lay person of the
realm, within franchise or without, both male and female and of
whatsoever estate or condition, who have reached the age of fifteen.

Parliament Rolls

Northampton, November 1380

Rain punished the thick walls of Northampton and turned the cold
stone slick. The thin streets of the busy little town should have been
full, but on a grey Thursday morning in early November 1380, it
was wet, chilly and quiet.

Inside a small chamber adjoining the Priory of St Andrew, tucked
away in the north-west corner of the town, the archbishop of
Canterbury gave a signal, and above the clattering of the downpour outside, a long and familiar reading began. The text was
Magna Carta, literally 'the great charter' of England's liberties. As
it filled the steaming room, the damp handful of lords, bishops
and gentlemen gathered together were reminded of the rights,
duties and responsibilities they held and exercised as England's
elite court and general council.

It was the first day of Parliament. Or rather, it was the second
first day. Parliament had been due to begin on Monday, but bad
weather had enforced a three-day delay. Still the numbers were thin.

These occasions were by tradition sparsely attended, but even by recent standards, this was a poor turnout. In the heart of the country, Northampton should have been an easy destination for everyone whose presence was required at Parliament. But that autumn had seen dark black skies and unrelenting, torrential storms, which had turned the roads into thick and dangerous furrows. Travel, always burdensome over long distances, became treacherous as rivers burst their banks and flooded England's well-trodden commercial thoroughfares.

Churchmen, laymen, nobles and their servants were all braving the elements to attend the realm's fifth parliament in just four years. The Crown's needs were so immediate and severe that even the thirteen-year-old king, Richard II, had struggled through the downpour to arrive a few miles away at the manor of Moulton. He was to lodge there for several months, surrounded by his household, his tutors and his boyhood companions, holding his court in unfamiliar surroundings while his countrymen attempted, on his behalf, to solve an impending national crisis.

The threat that faced the Crown and realm was clear and urgent. Peace with France – shaky throughout most of the century – had long since collapsed and the French, seeing a power vacuum at the head of English government, knew they had the upper hand. England's enemies scorned the notion that that the young king's government might be capable of reaching a fair and balanced settlement to the Hundred Years War. French and Spanish fleets terrorised the Channel, the Scots were raiding the northern borders, Ireland was turbulent, English garrisons on the Continent were impoverished and the nation had been on a defensive footing as it anticipated invasion from both land and sea for the last three and a half years. The south coast and the whole of southern England was in a state of heightened peril, and even Oxford – a couple of hundred miles inland – was planning for the worst, and nervously considering making improvements to its crumbling fortifications.

It was a measure of the severity of the crisis that Parliament had been called at all. January's tax, granted in a similarly thunderous

Westminster, had been hard, and the commons protested fiercely against what they saw as aristocratic financial incompetence. The deal they had brokered then was that the king could take his money, but had then to hold off for at least eighteen months before coming cap in hand again.[1] But the tax that had been granted there proved quite inadequate to the government's demands, and just months after Westminster had emptied of parliamentary attendees, an embarrassing repeat summons had been sent across the country to this new gathering in Northampton. Now the mood was one of marked reluctance to allow the cycle of waste and squander to continue.

With the best and most imposing noble lords from the January parliament all absent on campaign, Northampton was achingly short of good worshipful noblemen with the necessary grandeur to overawe and bully the commons into giving up their gold. Chief among them, the government missed John of Gaunt, the king's bullish, prickly uncle, the most powerful nobleman in all of England, and a man recognised as a major force in European politics by most of the western half of the Continent. Gaunt, out of necessity, was absent in the northern reaches of the realm, negotiating a peace treaty with Scotland. He was not expected in the Midlands until the end of the month.

But Parliament could not wait for him. So here sat the realm, on Thursday morning, in the refectory hall of St Andrew's Priory, patiently waiting for the formalities to finish and for Archbishop Simon Sudbury of Canterbury, Chancellor of England and the government's most senior official, to offer them his opening remarks.

He stood before them, an ageing, thoughtful and reserved Suffolk-born theologian, with all the burden of the troubled kingdom on his shoulders, and explained that the earl of Buckingham, the king's twenty-five-year-old uncle was, despite his military inexperience, now the leading general of the troops in France. He was there at that moment, together with a large number of 'other great lords, knights, squires, archers and other good men of the kingdom'.[2]

The king had assigned to Buckingham all the resources granted to him at the last parliament, and much of his own money, explained

Sudbury. Furthermore, because of debts Richard had incurred for the expedition to Scotland and the defence of royal subjects in the disputed territories of Gascony, not to mention the money due to the earl of March for the defence of Ireland, the council had pledged away most of Richard's royal jewels in security for vast and unserviceable cash loans, including many from wealthy merchants in the City of London. The ancient Plantagenet heirlooms and symbols of royal splendour were in danger of being lost.

There was worse, too. Sudbury went on to explain that owing to a rising in Flanders, the wool tax that creamed a reliable profit from merchants trading on the London cloth market was gone. The armies had been promised the advance of another six months' pay, and reinforcements of men and horses; the coasts of the southeast required massive and immediate investment to protect them against the relentless raids by Franco-Spanish fleets; the wages of soldiers in Calais, Brest and Cherbourg were more than nine months in arrears, to the point where the men were talking of desertion.

In short, warned Sudbury, this was going to be expensive. Though parliamentary protocol demanded that he asked the commons to 'advise' the king and to show him 'how and by what means you think these expenses may be best met with the least discomfort to yourselves',[3] it was clear that this was not a polite request for money, nor even a terse demand – it was a desperate plea for a lot of money, fast, and the devil care at what price.

Listening to Sudbury's speech was Sir John Gildesburgh, knight, war veteran and politician, and a man who had been at the heart of the Hundred Years War for as long as he could remember. War had shaped his life and earned him his fortune. He had fought alongside Prince Edward at Crécy in 1346, when he was fifteen and the prince only a year older. Gildesburgh's whole youth and young manhood were typical of a generation of landowning military gentlemen, whose lives had been absorbed by the brutal and bloody campaigns that dominated the years before Bretigny. Like many others, young Gildesburgh had won through his loyal service the grant of a manor, a lucrative marriage in Essex, and friendship with the county aristocracy.

In Parliament at Northampton now, twenty years after Bretigny, Sir John was learning to live by a different kind of sword. Here, Sir John did political battle in his role as parliamentary speaker – which he had performed at the last parliament – interpreting and voicing all of the commons' demands and opinions to the lords and to the king.

After Sudbury had made his opening remarks, Gildesburgh led the commons aside for a frank discussion. Like many of his fellows, he was torn in two directions. Gildesburgh was a knight of the shire, but he was also an ally of Buckingham. For many years he had shared personal interests with the other landowners in the commons, on whom the burden of regular taxation fell most frequently. But he also realised the gravity of the crisis, and the urgent need for a huge grant of taxation to keep the war afloat. To refuse the Crown's request for funds outright would almost certainly lead, before long, to a full-scale invasion by the French, which would bring devastating consequences to every man in Parliament – possibly heralding upheaval for landowners on a scale unseen since the Norman Conquest, when, within a generation, William the Conqueror's invaders had virtually eradicated the old Saxon landholding nobility, seizing their land for themselves.

Yet the commons felt unable to sustain a burden of taxation that weighed uncharitably heavy on their shoulders. True enough, at the previous parliament some of the burden of tax had been alleviated from the landowners in favour of milking the close relationship between the Crown and the powerful merchants of London. The city's super-rich merchants had bolstered a moderately heavy general property tax with vast loans set against the Crown jewels. In exchange, these merchant tycoons and leading London politicians such as William Walworth and John Philipot had secured for themselves posts on the panel that administered the money that poured into the treasury. Unfortunately, during the months that intervened, John of Gaunt had ridden roughshod over that agreement. So this time around

Gildesburgh knew as he addressed the damp and travel-weary parliamentary commons that Gaunt, with his remarkable capacity to offend and upset potential allies, had dashed any hope of repeating the last parliament's deal.

In the eyes of the parliamentary commons, there remained one class that was virgin territory, relatively untouched by tax: the labourers.

Even given the parlous state of royal finances, when the government revealed to the parliamentary commons just how much it needed to keep the war effort alive, the amount was astounding. The knights and burgesses had filed back from their dormitory to the dining room expecting a stiff demand, but they could not have anticipated the insane ransom that Sudbury demanded. The sum that was deemed fit to keep the country afloat was a staggering £160,000. It was eight times the sum that had been raised by the last major tax, in 1379.

It was, said the commons, completely 'outrageous', and utterly impossible. Now it was the turn of the lords and the Crown to deliberate. And, like the commons, the lords looked to the lower orders, a class that they saw every day on their estates becoming richer and more aware of the monetary value of their labour. Unsurprisingly, the same solution crept into their minds. This time, agreed the lords, the country might be able to spread the burden of paying for the war effort. If the parliamentary commons didn't want to pay for the whole effort themselves, then they could grant another poll tax.

Though there had been two poll taxes in the previous four years, neither had been imposed in the form that the November parliament conceived it. In 1378 every person in England aged over fourteen had been charged a groat (4d) – about a day's wages for a skilled craftsman, or two days' pay for a farmhand. This was not especially onerous. The net amount paid by most families was scarcely provocative and certainly not crippling. Communities were assessed en masse and generally left to divide the tax burden between themselves – which generally meant according to their means.

The second poll tax had taken this principle of the bill varying according to income and written it into law. There was a long, gradu-ated list of rates for every estate of man, from dukes to farmhands.

Now, though, the lords asked for a flat, universal tax to be levied of four or five groats (16d–20d) per person. They must have realised that even with the relatively new affluence of some parts of the English lower orders, this was a grotesque hike. The earlier poll taxes had been innovative, net-widening and moderately set. This was heavy, crude and blatantly devised to shift the burden of war funding away from the landed classes. However communities tried to spread the burden of payment, a poll tax at this level would cripple the weak and poor. It stood the ideal of Christian charity on its head, and even when the lords suggested that the tax be made fairer with a commitment to compel the strong to help the weak, it was, at this level, simply not fair.

The commons dug in their heels. At five groats per head, the lords' suggestion was downright scandalous; £160,000 was just too much, they said, presumably thinking of the stormy reaction they them-selves would receive back home if appointed as tax collectors. Asking even the relatively wealthy ordinary folk of the south-east to pay a week's wages for every adult member of their family invited resist-ance; if they were going to go out into the countryside and start emptying the pockets of the peasants, then they had to know some limits.

Negotiations reached an impasse. The commons went back to their chambers, and argued for days about the best way to proceed. There was no doubt of the urgency of the situation, and it was trouble-some to consider the ire that would rain down in private on men like Gildesburgh and all those like him who had private links with the lords should they fail to deliver a satisfactory grant. On the other hand, what the lords and Crown asked was preposterous – an intoler-able burden to place on the country at large.

Eventually they reached a compromise.

The commons agreed to grant £100,000, one third of which was to be paid by the clergy. The clergy wouldn't like it, reasoned Parliament, but they could afford it, and they were less likely to be difficult about finding the money than the lay folk in the country-side. Moreover, the commons must have known that this particular solution would find favour with the Crown – Gaunt and Buckingham were both known to harbour some sympathy for the radical theologian John Wyclif, who had been railing against the wealth and corruption of the English Church for years. They would not shirk from siphoning a little episcopal wealth in the name of national defence. The bishops and abbots in Parliament huffed and puffed and protested that Parliament was a wholly inappropriate institution to be extorting money from them, but their complaints were ignored.

Meanwhile, the labourers, on whom the principal burden would still fall, had no voice at all. They would bear the bulk of the cost of defending the realm, and contributing a greater share than ever before to the war effort.

By early December, the form of the tax had been thrashed out in full and formal terms. Two-thirds was to be collected from the common people immediately, with a further third to be collected by the summer. Mirror arrangements would be carried out to take an equivalent levy from the clerics.

If all went according to plan, and the tax-collecting commissions did their jobs, then by June 1381 the country would be safe, secure and peaceable once again. The next parliament – likely to be in a year's time – would be able to assemble back in London, and with any luck would not be plagued by the rain. A new and lucrative source of income would have been established, tapping into the wealth of the English lower orders.

Everything was looking up.

TWO

LANCASTER

During this crisis, the commons held the peaceful duke of Lancaster
as their most hated enemy of all mortal men and would certainly
have destroyed him immediately if they had found him . . .

HENRY KNIGHTON

As the Northampton parliament progressed, it would have occurred
to many who sat throughout the days of financial wrangling that
one man, and one man alone, was to blame for Parliament's strange
location outside its usual home of Westminster. That man was John
of Gaunt, the duke of Lancaster, and it was because of his long
and significant feud with the City of London, its common people and
citizens, that Parliament had moved.

There had been little love between the duke and the City for many
years. The common people thought him a tyrant, and the great
merchants who controlled the City's politics and trade saw him as
a dangerous enemy of their influence. They disliked Gaunt, and
resented his blunt meddling in City affairs. Inevitably, given the
shadow he cast over government, he received a disproportionate share
of personal blame for the disastrous conduct of the Continental wars
and the resulting threat to sea trading routes on the Continent and
around the English coast. The hatred percolated through the orders
of City folk, and the common multitude regarded the duke with
suspicion and contempt, and took any chance to rise against him.

Gaunt, for his part, lacked the common touch to win over the mob, resented the merchant oligarchs' close relationships with the king and despised the royal reliance on their finances.

During the decline and death of Edward III, and the infancy of the present King Richard II, relations had reached a woeful state. Gaunt had no firm power base in the City, yet could not resist dabbling in its politics. For all his smooth charm in the international arena, when it came to domestic politics Gaunt seems to have found it pathologically impossible to ignore an opportunity for trampling on his lessers. The result was a skein of disastrous instability in City governance, and a series of riots and risings leading up to the summer of 1381. The stunning palace of the Savoy, built on the wealthy riverside strip of affluent suburbia, had come to serve as a locus of discontent for hostile citizens and the urban mob.

One of the major sources of friction in London was Gaunt's unsubtle support for John Wyclif, the outspoken advocate of Church reform, who was regarded by many as a dangerous heretic. In February 1377 Gaunt had prompted rioting across the City by interfering in Wyclif's trial for heresy at St Paul's. William Courtenay, bishop of London, and a hugely influential figure across the well-steepled City, in which stood ninety-nine churches within the square mile of its walls, had been presiding over Wyclif's interrogation, and Gaunt had appeared in the cathedral in support of his protégé. The case drew enormous interest from the common populace, who were roughly split in their opinions of Wyclif, but who were united in their suspicion of the duke, not least because he was widely believed to be considering the appointment of a royal captain to govern the City, in place of a popularly elected mayor.

The case before a packed and turbulent St Paul's soon descended into a slanging match between duke and bishop, who raged at one another over an issue as trivial as whether Wyclif should stand or sit while the charges were read. And it erupted into chaos when Gaunt threatened to drag the indignant bishop out of the cathedral and all the way to Windsor by his hair.

Gaunt's arrogance prompted total outrage and the trial quickly dissolved into violence. After a day's protest a furious mob baying for Gaunt's head thronged out of the City walls at Ludgate, made their way for two miles along Fleet Street and the Strand and attacked the Savoy. Gaunt had the good sense to leave home before the mob appeared on his doorstep and had fled downriver so the Londoners had contented themselves with turning upside down Gaunt's coat of arms – the mark of a traitor. It was left to the humiliated Bishop Courtenay to bring the City to order.

Having thus offended London's clerical population, excited her common folk and united both sides against him on a generally divisive issue, Gaunt had the very next year contrived to involve himself in another, even more serious incident, which had a similarly grievous effect on City morale and stability. There had been another major conflagration, as the controversial knight Sir Ralph Ferrers had burst into Westminster Abbey during Mass, violated sanctuary and murdered both a sacristan and a squire, Robert Hawley, who had sought refuge there following his escape from the Tower of London. Ferrers was thought – wrongly – to be connected with, or under orders from, Gaunt, and though the duke was, in fact, in Brittany at the time of the outrage, he waded into the debate on his return, choosing to defend Ferrers' plainly appalling behaviour. Once again, he had inflamed tensions in London for the sake of imposing his own authority.

Yet again, there were protests, but Gaunt continued to meddle, and with his connivance, statutes were passed at the Gloucester parliament of 1378, stripping the fishmongers – one of the leading groups of merchants in London – of their trade monopolies and roles in national government: the richest and most powerful fishmonger, William Walworth, was removed from his position as war treasurer; the same treatment was afforded to the leading grocer in the City, John Philipot, who had contributed handsomely to the war effort not only via loans to the Crown, but also by chartering a private fleet of warships to protect the coast from Scottish pirates; and the earl of Buckingham had made a vehement speech attacking Nicholas Brembre, another of the greatest merchants in London and a close associate of Walworth and Philipot.

By summer 1379, the City had begun to develop something of a persecution complex. Rumour had started to spread of a plot, led by Gaunt, to strike still harder against London's ruling elites. It was said that the Genoan ambassador to England, Janus Imperial, was in negotiations with the Crown not just to secure favourable trading terms, but to move England's primary point of trade away from London. Speculation was rife that Southampton was to be made the new trading capital of the country, and that Gaunt and the Genoans were on the verge of brokering a deal that would break the London merchant oligarchs for good. In August, the merchants struck back: Imperial was brutally stabbed to death on the doorstep of his lodgings in St Nicholas Acon Street. John Kirkby and John Algor, a pair of small-time hoodlums selected from London's native trading guilds, were sent to pick a fight with the ambassador's servants, during the course of which Kirkby had stabbed the unfortunate ambassador twice in the head, killing him with two cuts to the skull, which the coroner described quite precisely as 'seven inches long and deep into the brain'.[1]

This was more than just a warning shot. Imperial was an ambassador to the Crown, protected by royal warrants of safe passage and evidently extremely well connected. Killing him was an act of lese-majesty – a wilful derogation of royal authority. Gaunt and the government strained every sinew to frame the case not simply as murder, but as treason. Forces in the City pressed hard on every investigating jury that was involved in the case to return no verdict, to resist the overtures to convict that were placed on them by judges, and generally to obstruct the case in every way possible.

Now the outcome was to be settled once and for all in a grand trial in Northampton. The result would be a serious boon for whichever party it favoured.

So, in early November 1380, Gaunt was heading south. He had spent late October and the first week of November in the chilly border-lands that buffered England from Scotland, negotiating peace between the realm of his nephew the king, and a deputation of Scottish lords.

Now, as rain tipped down out of a leaden sky, he was riding home to England.

He had reason to be proud of his achievements. The king's council had sent Gaunt north in late October as a trusted member of the court to squash the various petty northern squabbles that were threatening to erupt into an outbreak of serious violence. Trouble largely stemmed from pirates operating out of Hull and Newcastle, who had captured a Scottish ship. Sea-raiding was an occupational hazard for traffic in the North Sea, but on this occasion the Scots had reacted to the loss by breaching the border, terrorising the northern counties and looting Penrith. This was not an unusual occurrence, but the timing was bad, opening as it did another unwanted front in the war.

Gaunt, as the greatest landowner in the country, boasted territorial interests in every corner of England and Wales, from a castle in Northumberland to manors in south Devon; and fortresses and properties across the breadth of the country, from Carmarthen to East Anglia. Protecting the northern border certainly held some private interest for him; but he was also a champion of the rights of the Crown – a trait that often saw him unfairly characterised as having personal ambitions to the throne, but which made him a hugely effective ambassador in negotiating international settlements.

One of Gaunt's maxims in diplomacy was 'peace in time of peace, war in time of war'.[2] With the war coffers virtually empty, he had gone north to ensure that this remained a time of peace. The royal council had sent advance orders to restrain the belligerent local lord, Henry Percy, earl of Northumberland, from turning a squabble into a bloodbath, and Gaunt had been dispatched with sufficient military strength to subdue the enemy by force if necessary, but enough common sense to see the value of making peace, particularly when his own retinue contained a notable contingent of Scots.

On 8 November, Gaunt had completed his negotiations and left Newcastle with his retinue of soldiers, officials and servants. Conciliatory talks had ended with the agreement that neither side would invade for the next thirteen months. Gaunt had appointed officials to keep the peace on behalf of the Crown, successfully safeguarding his own small clusters of properties in Northumberland, Cumberland and County Durham from attack, as well as bringing peace to the realm at large. The northern border was secure, and Gaunt was free to turn his attentions to matters much farther south.

He had been content to leave the management of parliamentary taxation to lesser men than himself, but Gaunt was eager to get to Northampton before the proceedings at large were finished. He reached the town in time to see the end of the parliament, and to take his place at the head of a panel of nobles assembled to try Janus Imperial's alleged killers, Kirkby and Algor. He lined up with Richard, earl of Arundel, Thomas Beauchamp, earl of Warwick, Hugh Segrave, steward of the king's household, William Beauchamp, the king's chamberlain, and Sir John Burley, and on 3 December, Algor was brought before them to give evidence. He was questioned first because he was the more malleable of the two men. Either his conscience or the king's jailers had persuaded him to plea-bargain, so he came before the nobles not to fight his case, but to make a confession of his guilt, and to implicate his conspirators.

Algor, out of his depth and no doubt traumatised after a year in prison, did little more than rehearse the words Gaunt and the government wanted to hear. He explained what had happened when he and Kirkby had attacked Imperial's servants, accepting responsibility for deliberately stamping on the ambassador's feet, noting his own involvement in the knife fight, and blaming Kirkby for delivering the final wounds to Imperial. At this point his confession became political.

Algor implicated by association not only his master, Richard of Preston, but also the triumvirate of merchant oligarchs so troublesome to Gaunt: Brembre, Walworth and Philipot. Algor claimed Preston and Philipot had a financial interest in seeing Imperial killed, owing to an outstanding lawsuit between them, while Walworth and Brembre were identified as the owners of households in which anti-Genoan gossip and slander were rife. These were serious accusations, because Philipot was serving as mayor at the time of Imperial's murder, and had personally arrested Kirkby and Algor. Walworth and Brembre, on the other hand, were not being directly accused of treason, but were compromised by their inclusion in the confession and now knew that they were being closely watched. Their latitude to govern effectively within their own city had been publicly clipped, and though no direct blow had been struck, the taint of treason by association now hung over them.

Having fulfilled his side of the bargain, Algor was returned to prison, where he would remain until 1384. Kirkby was dragged before the court the next day, charged with his crime and condemned to a traitor's death. The sentence could not have been carried out in London, such was the outrage that it, and Algor's blatantly political confession, would have generated among the citizens. But in the neutral territory of Northampton, Kirkby was hanged, drawn and quartered. It was a satisfying victory for Gaunt over the Londoners, and it completed what, for the government, was a successful month in the provinces: peace had been made, political points scored and justice dispensed. Taxes had been granted and the impetuous native government in London had been very publicly slapped down.

Yet the short-term gains at Northampton stored up some very serious problems for the future. An inequitable tax that targeted relatively poor rural communities had been approved by a combination of a notoriously inept government and a landowning class that had the strongest interest in shifting the fiscal burden away from themselves. The only remedy for the constant harrying of the coast and the crippling disruption of trade had been to throw more money at the problems.

Furthermore, the City of London, where many of these problems crystallised most visibly, had suffered once again from John of Gaunt's destabilising influence. Determined to impose his personal authority, he had undermined a group of men who had ruling experience, private military means and sufficient private wealth to support the Crown when necessary. Instead of supporting their rule during a period of national insecurity, he had opened them up to attacks from their enemies within the City. The mayor, John Philipot – whose office was already under threat from Gaunt's desire to impose direct royal government on London – was now suffering under the implied taint of treachery, as were other influential citizens, including Walworth and Brembre. This encouraged political division in the City, especially among the lower orders and lesser citizens who grumbled against what they saw as the overweening influence of the merchant oligarchs. This in turn added to the uneasy mood felt among the common folk of London, while simultaneously inflaming their dislike of Gaunt himself.

All of these things would have serious repercussions the following summer. But as Parliament closed and Northampton emptied of its exalted visitors, none of that was known. For now, all that seemed to be necessary was to pack up, return to Westminster and begin the demanding task of collecting the poll tax.

THREE

COLLECTIONS

Because it seemed to various lords and the commons that these
subsidies had not been properly or honestly collected ... the royal
council appointed certain commissions to make inquiry in every
township how they had been levied ... [and] the said inquisitors much
provoked the people ...

HENRY KNIGHTON

Essex, May 1381

The prosperous market town of Brentwood was a familiar stop on
the busy trading road through Essex that connected London with
Colchester. Originally known as Burnt Wood, it was a relatively young
town, hacked out of the thick Essex woodland by the canons of Osyth
Priory in the 1170s. It was part of the county's diverse, healthy
economy, which was driven by (but by no means solely reliant on)
the wool trade with Flanders. Served by clusters of villages that were
dotted along the banks of the Thames estuary, Brentwood was a
natural hub for the county's traders. Many inhabitants of the economic-
ally busy and geographically mobile shire would have been familiar
with its streets, and with the market that drew together traders,
hawkers and farmers from across the shire on a regular basis.

On Thursday, 30 May, the town of Brentwood hummed with the
presence of several hundred such local villagers. The most senior
men from the rural settlements in and around the hundred of

Hinckford, including the villages of Fobbing, Corringham, Stanford, Mucking, Horndon, Billericay, Rawreth, Ramsden, Warley, Ginge, Goldhanger, Ingatestone and other places farther afield, had been summoned to town to participate in peace sessions before the county justices, led by Sir John Gildesburgh. Influential local men sat in judgement of the lesser, who mingled around the town in a state of taut anticipation.

On the surface, this was part of the familiar yearly ritual of medieval life. Late May and early June was a time of business and merrymaking in England. It was a time of popular religious observance, with the festivals of Whitsun, Trinity and Corpus Christi following closely upon each other, giving rise in the villages and towns to fairs, festivals, pageants, processions and 'summer games' – social rituals of playful mischief and controlled disorder, where labourers played at being lords and the lords tried to bear it all with good humour. This year there was added tension: a great storm had blown up earlier in the month, exciting and stirring the lower orders, and sending a portentous crackle through the air.

Whitsun, which was to be celebrated on the coming weekend, was a familiar time of official administration. The central law courts in Westminster were on vacation, and the royal justices made their routine county visits. Manorial courts – private law courts held by local landowners – also held their sessions, at which they would take views of frankpledge – oaths from all the adult males in their jurisdiction that they would agree to keep their tithing (little arrangements of ten or so households) in good order, and present any misdemeanours before the court. All in all, it was a busy time, at which men and women congregated, communicated and travelled through the local area – the perfect time for mobilising large groups of people.

Between Christmas 1380 and Whitsun 1381 Essex and every other county in England had grown used to seeing the members of royal commissions. Almost as soon as the Northampton parliament had granted the tax, collectors had been appointed right across the country, to take receipt of the money gathered by individual communities.

There had been a strange ferocity about the government's demands. What had not been revealed to the Northampton parliament about the huge sum demanded was that it was to fund not one but two military tasks. The first was indeed the sustenance of the earl of Buckingham's French front; but the second was to equip an entirely new army to be sent to Portugal. John of Gaunt had grand territorial designs on Castile, and by his insistence a fleet was to be equipped in May under his brother, Edmund Langley, earl of Cambridge.

With such huge obligations to fulfil, a new treasurer had been appointed on 1 February. Direction of the exchequer had been handed over to Sir Robert Hales, prior of the Hospital of St John of Jerusalem, and owner of several fine estates in Essex and Hertfordshire.

Throughout February, Hales had carried out 'viewings', or audits, of the tax receipts. They were grim, riddled with evasion. In Essex, which had declared a taxable population of nearly 48,000 in 1377, the eligible folk of the county now claimed to number just 30,748. Similar numbers were reported all across the country. To believe the returns, it would seem that the population across the whole of the south-east had fallen between 20 and 50 per cent in the space of two years. In the century of the Black Death, this was not unprecedented – but as there had been no serious outbreaks of plague in recent years, it was clear that those villages and towns that were declaring a depleted population and paying an accordingly reduced tax bill were engaged in blatant fraud.

The main tactic was to refuse to acknowledge unmarried females. Widows, sisters and daughters levied a burden on communities which they could not make good by work, so it made sense to exclude them from the community levy, especially if they were new additions to the tax roll, when their inclusion seemed the most unjust.

By mid-March the government had reached the limit of its patience. The members of the king's council were furious, and blamed corruption and dishonesty on the part of the collectors and the leading figures in the localities. The response – quickly rumoured to be at the behest of a royal householder and serjeant-at-arms, John Legge – was to launch royal commissions of inquisition to go into the countryside and find out what was happening.

These commissions were dispatched under orders to 'investigate and inspect' copies of the original assessments, and compare their findings with 'oaths of the constables and bailiffs of each vill and borough' as to the true number of eligible taxpayers lurking undeclared. They were commanded to extract in full the shortfall, and pay it into the exchequer. The date for final payment of the entire £66,666 lay tax contribution was dragged forward from 2 June to 21 April.

So it was that counties like Essex and towns like Brentwood had been subjected to a second round of government interference in their lives. The inspecting commissions quickly gained a reputation for ugly methods. Their official instructions also commanded them to 'seize and arrest all those whom you find acting in opposition or rebellion to the above commands'; such men were 'to be held in ... prisons where they are to stay until we make provision for their punishment'. Muscle was provided to each commission in the form of a pair of royal serjeants-at-arms assigned to travel with them. Serjeants-at-arms – such as Legge – were effectively royal thugs, heavily armed members of the king's bodyguard who expected to intimidate with their might and worship as members of the royal household, and – frequently – their sheer physical size.

Ill feeling spread fast. Rumours circulated concerning the harsh and disrespectful methods of the commissioners. Word spread that in one village (after the revolt the tradition sprang up that it was Fobbing, an Essex estuary village close to Brentwood) a commissioner 'shamelessly lifted the young girls' skirts to test whether they had enjoyed intercourse with men'.[1] This would make them liable for taxation, but it was not a test to which any decent parent would consent – 'many would rather pay for their daughters than see them touched in such a disgraceful way'.[2]

Possibly as a result of their apparently gleeful heavy-handedness, it was also rumoured that the government was trading in poll tax commissions, by allowing court favourites to buy a licence to collect the tax shortfall, and keep any profits above what was owed to the exchequer for themselves. Whether any of this was true or not, it is clear that the aggression and contempt shown towards the villagers of the south-east by certain zealots on the tax commissions were provocative in the extreme, and in protest against what the chronicler Henry Knighton summed up as 'the imposition of new and almost unbearable burdens which appeared to be endless and without remedy', the people of the region began to conceive of a plan to resist.

Just such a plan had been gestating in Essex for some time. In all of the incursions into the shires, royal government was represented by familiar local faces from the gentry landowning class. In Essex the three most prominent were Sir John de Gildesburgh, Sir John de Bampton, a former sheriff and royal steward, and Sir John Sewale, the sheriff of Essex. Since the later years of Edward III's reign all three had been active in transacting royal business in the county. Bampton was a particularly notorious figure. In 1377 he had been one of the panel appointed to oversee the recruitment and training of archers and men-at-arms to resist invasion, and to provide for beacons to be lit across the county in the horrible event that the French landed. The following year he had been appointed a JP. In March, Gildesburgh and Sewale had sat on the panels to investigate the paltry returns that had reached the exchequer in payment for the third poll tax. Now Bampton and Gildesburgh returned at the head of peace commissions. Though these were regular events in the judicial calendar, to the majority of people in Brentwood their nominal purpose was immaterial. These were simply more royal commissions, making more punitive incursions into Essex life. A whisper of resistance went around.

Those men who gathered for the 30 May peace sessions in the town were there to represent their villages. As such, they included men of some local seniority, many of whom could claim to be representative of the interests and ideas of the broad mass of those with whom they lived and worked. Villager after villager would have spoken of their frustration with the incessant demands and interference of the machinery of royal justice; its lack of equity, and the misgovernment of the realm in the name of an innocent young king. That sentiment, allied with the mischievous spirit of the season and the electric foreboding that had come with the storms, had manifested itself in a readiness to resist and rebel – to stand against Gildesburgh, Bampton, Sewale and all those like them.

As the day's peace sessions progressed, Bampton and Gildesburgh called before them various representatives of the villages in Hinckley.

Fobbing, represented by a man called Thomas Baker, was a village in high foment. During the days leading up to 30 May, Baker had '[taken] courage and beg[u]n to exhort and ally himself with the men of his village. These men leagued themselves with others and in turn they contacted their friends and relations so that their message passed from village to village and area to area.'[3]

We do not know what business Bampton called Baker forward on, but it was assumed afterwards that it was connected with the earlier poll tax investigations. Our main source records that, sitting there in his pomp, Bampton commanded Baker and his associates to make on behalf of Fobbing 'a diligent enquiry [into tax evasion], give their reply and pay their money'.[4] Baker's men, who had been waiting, no doubt nervously, for this moment, 'replied that they would pay nothing at all',[5] arguing that Bampton himself had just months earlier accepted their previous payment – which made his current commission little more than a thinly veiled excuse for yet another new tax.

Bampton was taken aback by the insolence. He snapped back with a threat and a pointed reference to the armed serjeants that flanked him. But numbers and solidarity between the different sets of villagers all assembled in Brentwood made the Fobbing men bold. Bampton's tartness served not to subdue but to embolden them and their allies from all the other villages gathered in the town. As a mob, more than a hundred villagers told Bampton outright 'that they would not deal with him nor give him any money'.[6] Knighton later recorded that they were 'delighted that the day had come when they could help each other in the face of so urgent a necessity'.

Livid at this display of insubordination, Bampton ordered his bodyguards to arrest the malefactors. By the letter of his commission it was a reasonable demand. But realistically, he was being absurd. Two serjeants were ample to deal with a couple of recalcitrant defendants, but against a mob they were useless. The commons advanced menacingly towards the two increasingly pathetic serjeants and the entire commission realised their lives were in jeopardy. The villagers were armed – rudely, but capably – and Bampton's party fled, heading for home before their throats were slit. They rode hard south-west along the road back to London, bound for the royal council, their tails between their legs and a hail of arrows from the contemptuous mob following swiftly behind them.

Out of a mixture of frustration, belligerence and resentment, the first blow of the irate lower orders against what they saw as the overzealous and pompous agents of an incapable government had been struck. The village rebels disappeared into the forest that surrounded the town. As the night set in, the first band of rebels to have taken arms shivered beneath the trees. When the sun rose on the first day of June, the Great Revolt had begun.

FOUR

A CALL TO ARMS

> The commons took to the woods, for fear that they had of [Sir John Bampton's] great malice. They hid there for some time, until they were almost famished; and afterwards they went from town to town inciting other people to rise against the great lords and good men of the country.
>
> Anonimalle Chronicle

Whitsun 1381

Brentwood brought everything that had been hidden into the open. Many things that had been secret in the hearts and whispers of ordinary men were now known. Having driven Gildesburgh and Bampton from town with bows, arrows and volleys of violent threats, the angry crowd, realising that what was done was serious and dangerous, scrambled for the thickets and leafy anonymity of the woods. One set of royal officials had been sent packing, but there were more crawling around the county. Before long they would return, seeking retribution, punishment and bloodshed.

But the woods were no place for ordinary folk to live, and after nightfall hunger drove the rebels back on to the roads and into the open. The next day they began to venture back to their villages to report to their kinsmen and neighbours the detail of what had happened. The response far and wide throughout the villages along the estuary was common determination that what had started should not be an isolated flare-up, but the beginning of a county-wide rebellion against the constant encroachments of oppressive royal justice and the impositions of lordship.

But there was no real model for ordinary English villagers seeking to mobilise large-scale protest against the established order of lordship and justice. The county had to be raised by improvised methods. So the rebels began, said the Anonimalle chronicler, to go 'from place to place to stir up other people to rise against the lords and great folk of the country'. Men, almost certainly on horseback, given the speed of the rising, were sent out from village to village, proclaiming the start of a movement and whipping up rebellious fervour.

The leader of the first rebel company, which drew its followers from across the hundred of Barstaple, was Thomas Baker. Lurid rumours swept around of his personal motives: the chroniclers heard suggestions that he had been the avenging father whose daughter was molested by the hands of the tax inspectors. Perhaps that was true. What is certain is that he was a man of resolution and organisational skill, and well connected in Essex, Kent, Suffolk and Hertfordshire.

Soon the names of Baker and Fobbing were known across Essex, as runners and riders passed news of the movement he directed for miles around. They found like-minded men both in north Essex, close to Colchester, and south, beyond the broad Thames estuary, in Kent.

In Brentwood, Baker had been in contact with men from Bocking, a village comparable in size to Fobbing, situated farther north, in Hinckford hundred. The Bocking men would have carried back with them enthusiastic reports of Bampton and Gildesburgh's humiliating defeat, and they too began to move out into the county and spread the message of open insurrection. Village by village, the whole county began to move.

By Whitsun – Sunday, 2 June – it was clear that there were hundreds of willing men and women throughout Essex who would stand together and advance what had begun. This raised some practical questions. Clearly, it would not do simply to have the county plunged into anarchy. There was a clear and present need for structure.

So, as Bocking prepared to celebrate Whitsun, the village filled with men. Eight villages within a 10-mile radius sent representatives: Coggeshall and Stisted to the south-east; Braintree and Dunmowe to the south-west; and Ashen, Dedham, Little Henny and Gestingthorpe, all to the north or north-east. All would have come knowing the symbolism of their meeting place. Bocking had a long history as a place where the lower orders had attempted to resist the legal impositions of their manorial overlords. Sixty years earlier their ancestors had pursued a long legal battle with the priors of Christ Church, Canterbury, to try to wriggle free of some of the burdensome feudal obligations that came attached to their land and lives. Rich in this history of determined independence, it was a fitting meeting-place in 1381.

A large meeting was convened. There were no minutes, and what was said is lost, but a later legal case would allege that it was here that the assembled villagers rose 'treacherously against the lord king'. As a mark of the general commitment to what was sure to be a dangerous and perhaps fateful undertaking, all swore oaths to work together with one aim: 'to destroy divers lieges of the lord king and to have no law in England except only those they themselves moved to be ordained'. With that, the foundations for the county rebellion were laid.

It was very likely agreed at Bocking who constituted legitimate targets of the rebellion, and the methods by which recruits could be gathered. All men present agreed to catch and kill royal ministers and officials, and those whom they held responsible for the dismal governance of the country and the perceived corruption of justice that had repeatedly been visited on the common folk of the country, most recently by the poll tax commissions. First among these targets was Sheriff Sewale. Others included all those who had exercised positions of royal government or onerous private lordship in the county. Woe betide anyone who counted in both categories.

Violent coercion was also approved as a legitimate part of the recruitment drive. One observer wrote that the rebels 'went to the manors and townships of those who would not rise with them, and cast their houses to the ground or set fire to them'.[1] According to Thomas Walsingham, the St Albans chronicler, 'men of just two villages' – Fobbing, perhaps also Bocking – had

made it their business to send with all haste to every village, however small. Their aim was to get both the old and those men in their prime to join them equipped with such weapons as they could muster, allowing no excuses at all, so that those who refrained from joining them, and those who refused or disdained to do so, would know that they would have their possessions pillaged, their homes burned down or demolished and themselves be executed.

The revolt was cast from the outset as a community rebellion – and there was a 'with us or against us' mentality that had dire consequences for those opposed.

Bocking reflected the model of rebel organisation – sworn chapters or companies of men banded together by oath, led by the natural leaders of village society, in close communication with other bands of rebels and working to a common timetable – which revolved around strategic, coordinated strikes on selected targets. And as such the rural revolt can be seen not as a spontaneous, itinerant riot, but a carefully choreographed orgy of violence and retribution.

At the same time as the Whitsunday conventicles in Bocking were starting a month's rioting across Essex, the spirit of disorder was ghosting across the Thames and into Kent. Whitsun weekend had become a time for banding together, committing to the movement and readying the country community to rise as one. So communication began between the men in and around Barstaple hundred and the inhabitants of Dartford, which was one of the larger towns on the south bank of the estuary.

The prominent figure in this early stage of the Kent rebellion was Abel Ker, an inhabitant of Erith, a small port village just upstream from Dartford, south of Fobbing, with close links to London through the trading traffic of the river. Ker, like Thomas Baker, was a prominent enough member of local society to command the respect and deference of his peers. On Whitsunday, he gathered together a sizeable band of villagers from Erith and from Lesnes, a couple of miles west along the river, and took them to the nearby Augustinian abbey of St Mary and St Thomas the Martyr.

The abbey of Lesnes, like many other abbeys about England, was well endowed with land both in its own county and those surrounding it. Monastic communities tended to find themselves frequently in dispute with their tenants, and there was widespread ill feeling towards their use of their own courts to squeeze as much in the way of convenient labour services and feudal dues from their tenants as they could get away with. Lesnes had been a sloppily run institution throughout most of its recent history, with monastic discipline reaching a low point in the 1340s, when the Crown had had to be enlisted to help arrest vagabond and apostate monks. The abbot in 1381, William de Hethe, was obviously marked by men in the Dartford area as a prime example of bad lordship.

Hethe was at home when Ker's band bundled their way into the abbey. The rebels stormed in and took him hostage. They forced him to swear an oath in which he promised to be of the rebels' company, a prospect that no doubt terrified him to the limit of his wits, but which was marginally preferable to death at the hands of an angry mob.

The capture of the abbot was, for Ker's rebels, an impressive coup – regardless of the fact that his oath (and the *mea culpa* that it implied) was made under duress. It held enormous propaganda value, and to a degree it legitimised their actions about the county. The policy of forcing their social betters to profess support for the rising soon became a motif of the rebellion at large, which tells us something important about the rebel mindset: they aimed not to overturn or transform society, but to correct it from the top down.

Encouraged by his success at Lesnes, the next day – Whit Monday – Ker gathered together a small group from his conventicle and (presumably in a convoy of fishing boats) crossed the Thames to enter Essex. Assize sessions were due in Dartford under Sir Robert Belknap, Chief Justice of the Court of Common Pleas. Belknap was one of the two most senior judges in the country, and the prospect of answering to him for the attack on Lesnes Abbey and thus bringing to an end the successful protest after a single day held no appeal.

So Ker took his band over the river to Rainham, another small village, about ten miles west of Fobbing, to gather new recruits. His men spent the day raising and swearing into Ker's allegiance more than a hundred men from villages spread across southern Essex. Besides the ordinary villagers, Ker had specific targets for recruitment. He specifically targeted William Berland, a serving justice of the peace who had been an assessor for the 1379 poll tax. Ker's methods were not subtle: he coerced as his recruiting agent one William Chaundeler of Prittlewell, a seafront village in Rochford hundred, out in the eastern islands of Essex. Chaundeler later claimed to have been forced against his will to instruct Berland and John Prittlewell Senior to rise and meet the rebels at Rainham. Whether they got their men or not is unclear, but by the morning of Tuesday, 4 June, Ker had managed to summon a sizeable force of both Essex and Kent men, all sworn by solemn oath to the rebel cause, one or two of them probably in fear for their lives. They crossed back into Kent and readied themselves for Belknap.

Sir Robert Belknap was not merely a senior judge. He was a career lawyer who had been a favourite with both the royal court and with John of Gaunt from the early 1370s. Belknap was a familiar figure across the whole of the south-east, but not a popular one – those men who knew a little of London's politics would have been aware of the contempt in which London's populace held him. During Richard II's coronation ceremony the citizens had erected a likeness of his head on a water conduit along the route of the parade, so that all who passed would see him spewing wine out of his ridiculous mouth.

On Wednesday, 4 June, he arrived in Dartford on his regular

Whitsun assize duty. He had been in Stratford, not far from London, on the day that Bampton and Gildesburgh were chased from Brentwood, and during his subsequent scheduled visits to Barnet, in Hertfordshire, and then down to Southwark, the famous first staging post on the pilgrims' road to Canterbury, he would have heard the frantic reports coming back from Essex and Kent of the disorder that was spreading through the country. There must have been some advance word of his mood, because when it was learned that he was soon to arrive in Dartford at the scene of Ker's arm of the rebellion, there was such consternation that people across the countryside were said to have proposed abandoning their homes in fear.

But even with as grand a judge as Belknap at its head, fear of the law was quickly subsumed beneath popular anger against it. When the judicial train arrived at Dartford, the town dissolved into rioting. The chroniclers recall how 'the commons rose against [Belknap] and came before him to tell him that he was a traitor to the King, and that it was of pure malice that he would put them in default . . . And they took him, and made him swear on the Bible that never again would he hold such a session, nor act as a judge in such inquests.'[2]

The nonchalant tone belies a quite remarkable feat – one of the grandest judges in the country bewildered into submission by a band of rogues armed with recommissioned farm tools. Belknap, like Bampton before him, beat a hasty retreat.

From the chronicles next comes a sense of unstoppable disorder – the flashpoint in Brentwood spreading like flames through tinder, and erupting into a fire that consumed the whole of the south-east of England. In fact, during the first ten days of June the rebels' progress was phenomenally coherent, well organised and purposeful, as they unleashed a campaign aimed against agents of central government in the shires, and finally the national government itself. In south Essex, the Brentwood and Fobbing rebels continued to travel the county, raising villages, organising new sworn chapters or rebels, ensuring the coherence of the revolt and spreading the word that on Thursday, 6 June, the rebellion was to begin in earnest. It seemed that the authorities were powerless. Their usual monopoly of violence and control had been suddenly, ruthlessly broken by a group of ordinary working folk operating with an astounding level of organisation and coherence, and with a penchant for gruesome, summary dispensation of natural justice.

The first thing that each new village saw as the leading Kent rebels visited during that week was three gory standards. As Belknap was chased from the county, he had been compelled to give up the names of the jurors that had informed him of the perpetrators of the first Brentwood rising on 30 May. The rebels had tracked down three of them, severed their heads from their bodies and stuck them on poles. The bloody trophies went everywhere the rebel companies rode, their blackened, decaying features a warning: the time to rise had come, and the cause must be heeded.

FIVE

A GENERAL AND A PROPHET

> The Kentishmen, hearing of things most of them already desired,
> without delay assembled a large band of commons and rustics in the
> same manner as the men of Essex: in a short time they stirred up
> almost the whole province to a similar state of tumult.
>
> THOMAS WALSINGHAM

Kent

By Thursday, 6 June, all of Essex and Kent was in uproar. Voices
declaring for the rebellion pealed, with the urgency of church bells,
from village to village, and the rule of law began to dissolve into the
rule of rough rebel justice.

The rash of congregations and troublemaking took the authorities by surprise. The Crown had no army ready in the south-east.
The nearest significant military force had left London in early May
on a new, northern mission, once more commanded by Gaunt. It
was now far away in the borders, insurance against the failure of the
latest round of peace talks with the Scots.

Without the threat of royal military intervention, and increasingly
defiant of the authority of any travelling legal commissions, rebel
bands took to the roads in great numbers. They crossed county
borders and opened lines of communication between the now
numerous fringes of the revolt. Adding fuel to the flames, two London
butchers, Adam Attewell and Roger Harry, were riding throughout

Essex and the City's hinterlands, informing the rebel bands organising in the villages that if they came to London they could count on the support of urban allies.

The Londoners had their own grievances, and though they were not exactly the same as the provincial rebels', there were factions in the City who understood that inciting and stirring the lower orders in the countryside might provide a useful mask of disorder for them to settle some scores of their own – not least against property belonging to the absent Gaunt.

But before they considered any move on London, there were targets closer to home for the shire rebels to consider. On 6 June, a mob formed in Coggeshall, a village near Colchester in the north of the county. Coggeshall was home to Sheriff Sewale. Like all other representatives of judicial authority in the county, Sewale was now in grave danger.

For reasons best known to himself, as rebellion ripped through his county, Sewale had remained at home, and on 6 June he was barricaded, terrified, in his house next to the village chapel with Robert de Segynton, an exchequer clerk. A detachment of men from Bocking arrived in Coggeshall. There was a serious commotion. As the mob swelled outside the house, inside the two men grew desperate. The rebels made a barrage of hot threats against Sewale, which intimidated him so much that he thought seriously neither of raising arms against the rebels, nor of leaving his house. He simply sat inside, petrified, as outside the air rang with sinister promises of vengeance.

Throughout Essex, other members of the higher judicial and administrative class shivered at home in anticipation of the arrival of the same terror. The rebels had a specific list of victims. It included Sewale, Gildesburgh and Bampton, as well as men like Walter Fitzwalter, who had acted as deputy to the office of the constable of England, Thomas Mandeville, William Berland, Geoffrey Dersham, a royal manor steward, Thomas Tyrell, the Chief Justice, Robert Belknap, Clement Spicer and Robert Rikeden. All of these men had been peace commissioners, they were significant landowners in the county and had performed some judicial or administrative role in it.

To a man they were marked out for attacks on their property and, if possible, their persons.

Rebel policy across the river in Kent was a bit different. Abel Ker, with his advance party of Essex recruits and early risers from Kent, based himself at Dartford. Having hounded Belknap out of the county, and encouraged two days of widespread vandalism and rioting, they proceeded to ride out and begin agitating in villages within a 10-mile radius of the town. On 5 June they had banded together in the town and identified their target for a 6 June strike: Rochester Castle.

As the rebels flooded down towards Rochester, along the course of the old Roman road that cut down into the Medway villages and off towards Canterbury, they would have seen Rochester Castle looming: a huge, square fortress with an imposing Norman keep that had made a convenient prison since the twelfth century. King John had besieged it in the thirteenth century, digging mines beneath its walls then using burning pig fat to cause such a violent fire that a corner of the castle had collapsed. But by the late fourteenth century it had been repaired and occupied an important strategic position on both the London road and the Medway river. It should have been a bastion of county authority, and pretty much impenetrable, as the keep had walls 12 feet thick. It was a difficult target, built to keep prisoners in and invaders out.

The Kent peasants may have been organised, but they were not set up to wage siege warfare. Their ambition, however, made up for their lack of coercive means. Relying on their ability to cause panic, rather than their capacity to breach stone defences, they descended on the castle.

The irreverent lawlessness in the villages around the castle must either have infected or intimidated the castle's guards, for without the suggestion of a struggle, they simply gave up their posts. A mob opened the castle jail, and freed the prisoners that were kept there. And to the band of felons they added another, even more valuable trophy: the castle's keeper, Sir John Newton, was taken hostage.

The addition of a noble hostage to their ranks swelled the confidence of the rebels, and a party splintered off from Rochester and made their way to Maidstone. All around and behind them, there was organised tumult. The Roman road had been effectively closed off to anyone who would not swear to be of rebel company. This paralysed a vital communication route in the south-east, as this busy thoroughfare was the direct road leading from London to Canterbury – in whose cathedral the relics of St Thomas à Becket made the town one of the most famous pilgrim sites in the country. The fall of the Roman road isolated the capital and royal government from any potential loyalists in the south-east. Anyone passing along the road was liable to be stopped and commanded to take an oath of loyalty to the rebel cause, to be faithful to King Richard and the true commons, to accept no king called John (a sign of hatred for Gaunt),[1] to agree that they would be ready to rise with the rebels when summoned, and to pledge to convert as many of their neighbours to the same way of thinking as they could.

Even among the chaos and rioting, then, a clear statement of ideology was emerging. The rebels fixated on the cult of kingship, but despised all those dripping poison into the king's ear and spreading rot through the timber of government by their self-serving use of royal positions and power. And they saw themselves as the voices of true moral justice, on a mission to restore the natural order of things to the realm. They were the true commons indeed.

And they knew their targets well. Maidstone contained property belonging to William Topclyve, one of those who had sat in judgement with Belknap at Dartford. He had an impressive house at the Mote that was an ostentatious symbol of the wealth and status he held as the archbishop of Canterbury's steward and an important royal administrator. The rebels demonstrated their contempt for Topclyve and his class by joining with a party of excited townsfolk, running rampant through the building and razing it to the ground.

Most important of all, by the time the rebels reached Maidstone, they had gained two important leaders. Of everything that took place in the hours after the fall of Rochester Castle, the most significant was the rise to power of John Ball and Wat Tyler.

They were totally different in character and neither of them native to Kent, but Tyler and Ball were definitive of the subsequent events of the revolt. Tyler was an Essex man, probably from Colchester, who had settled in Maidstone and seems to have known Kent well. Possibly he had fought in the ranks of one or more of the English armies that had been taken to the Continent in previous years, for he certainly had the ability to marshal, muster and command a disparate band of recruits on long marches and flash raids. He may well have been behind the remarkably mature command that went out early in the Kent revolt instructing anyone that lived within 12 leagues of the sea to remain in the villages for defence of the coasts against possible French invasion.[2] He was a bold and inspirational general who seemed to leave a mark on many of those who came into contact with him. Certainly he outshone the other petty generals of the early stages of the revolt, for during the day that the rebels spent in Maidstone, he rose from an inconspicuous figure among many who joined in the rapine and plunder, to the overall commander of the riots.

His first major act, as Maidstone fell, was to raid the prison, and release Ball.

John Ball was a preacher, a poet, a maverick thinker and a natural rabble-rouser. He had been known to the Church, the secular authorities and the common people of the south-east for the best part of twenty years. Originally a priest in York, he had been imprisoned three times by the archbishop of Canterbury for being an incessant, heretical nuisance, preaching in churchyards and in public places across the region, railing against inequality, the corruption of the established Church and the tyrannies of the powerful against the powerless. His philosophy was in total defiance of medieval orthodoxy, and he had long been a thorn in the side of Archbishop Sudbury, under whose jurisdiction he practised much of his mischief. The archbishop had tried to subject Ball to everything from imprisonment to excommunication. If anything, this drove him to greater irreverence. By the time he was released from Maidstone, Ball had developed an ideology that called for an end to lordship in whatever form it could be found. In his enemies' eyes, his radical egalitarianism meant an end to all 'lords, archbishops, bishops, abbots, priors as well as most of the monks and canons so that there should be no bishop in England except for one archbishop, namely himself'.[3]

Tyler and Ball in combination were a dangerous prospect: the captain and the prophet; military nous married to popular demagogy. Together they provided a military and a visionary hub for rebels to cluster around. As support swelled for them, they picked up a travelling following, who moved between towns with them, but they also had a catalytic effect on villagers and townsmen all along the pilgrim road.

From Maidstone, Tyler's men marched back across the Kent Downs to the road, and during the weekend of 8 and 9 June they made their way to Canterbury. Trouble flared all the way along the road, as the rebels hunted for royal officials, servants of Gaunt and county administrators. They were looking out for men such as Thomas de Haselden, the controller of John of Gaunt's household, and Sir Thomas Osgrave, the sub-treasurer of England, and Nicholas Herring, an escheator, JP, poll tax investigator and steward of the king's lands in the county. Having a considerable contingent of Essex men among them, who may have known of the attacks that had begun against Sir John Sewale, they also had their sights set on William Septvantz, the sheriff of Kent.[4] And, of course, there was also petty plunder. A horse was seized back at Chalk, and the nearby town of Gravesend was incited to riot. Without the castle to provide a looming figure of authority, and with Sir John Newton sequestered to the rebel ranks, the area around Rochester remained chaotic. Fires and riots spread across the countryside, the air alive with smoke and fury. All the way from Rochester to Canterbury, villages began to burn. In Frindsbury, a house was set on fire, and a little way east along the pilgrim road, to the south of the Isle of Sheppey, there was further uproar. Houses were destroyed in the small market town of Sittingbourne, and one John Godwot was killed in Borden, a village about half a mile away. In Faversham, where the road began to cut through the woods on its approach into Canterbury, rioting caused damage to a limeworks.

Wat Tyler's men marched through the chaos, adding to it and inciting it as they went until, just before noon on Monday, 10 June, they arrived in the city of Canterbury. The city was ready for them.

Meanwhile, in Essex, Monday, 10 June was also marked as a day of decisive action. As in Kent, separate gangs coalesced into great mobs, with the aim of decapitating royal government in any sense they could.

Bands of rebels from all across Essex and northern Kent converged at nearby Cressing Temple. This was the site of the wealthy and imposing Hospitallers' estates, and as such was naturally associated with the Church, the landowning class in the county and the mis-government of the country at large – for the prior of the Hospitallers, Sir Robert Hales, was also England's treasurer. The rebels descended on the Cressing estates and sacked the manor. They stole armour, vestments, gold and silver, burned books, helped themselves to the food victualled there and drank three casks of wine. Then they pulled the building to the ground and set fire to it.

They could have smelled the smoke in Coggeshall, just three miles to the east. There, Sheriff Sewale was still at home, barricaded behind his door since before the weekend. As he quivered inside, men pushed into the village. There were representatives from at least forty different settlements terrorising the inhabitants. Some went to the abbey and raided it for muniments and charters – but others went to Sewale's house. This time threats were not enough. Sewale was not as lucky as he had been on 6 June. His house was overrun. He was beaten up and his clothing torn, and the house relieved of any official documents that the rebels could find. Sewale escaped with his life, but the escheator of Essex, John Ewell, was not so lucky: he was captured in Coggeshall and murdered.

With the sheriff of Essex toppled, royal power was symbolically extinguished. The next day the rebels moved on to Chelmsford, where there was a ceremonial burning of royal records in the streets. Anything with green sealing wax attached – the sign of a financial document – was given special attention. From that point on, the rebel gangs split back into their component parts, fanning out through the county and beyond in the pursuit of disorder and adventure.

Down in Kent, events were taking an even more serious turn.

Tyler's men entered Canterbury before noon. It seemed that there were thousands of them, pouring into the city with the momentum of a weekend's rioting behind them. High mass was under way in the cathedral when the rebels arrived. Evidently still keenly disciplined by Tyler, they knelt before the monks and then called on them to elect one of their number to be archbishop, 'for he who is archbishop now [i.e. Sudbury] is a traitor, and will be beheaded for his iniquity'.[5]

Their next action was to summon before them the mayor, bailiffs and citizens of the town and force them to take oaths of faith and loyalty to 'King Richard and the true commons'. Then the rebels demanded to know the names of any traitors in the town. Three names were handed over, and the victims were dragged out of their houses and beheaded in the street.

The vicious riots that began with the murders of these supposed traitors would consume Canterbury for the best part of the next month. There was fertile ground in the city in which rebellion could take root: urban government had been riven by faction and royal administrators had suffered attempts to obstruct their business for the past three years. Now many suffered violence, ruin and death. They included William Medmenham, whose property was targeted all over the county, and John Tebbe, a former bailiff and MP who had served on royal commissions in the 1370s. Medmenham's house was vandalised and stripped of its goods – and Tebbe was murdered. John Tece, a manorial official and another former bailiff, was also killed, and houses belonging to various other lords, including Sir Richard de Hoo, Thomas Garmwenton and Sir Thomas Fog, were plundered. All across Canterbury, Tyler's rural army joined with the artisans and servants of the city in delivering it into chaos.

In Canterbury, just as in Rochester, the fall of the castle was the principal sign of the rebels' dominance. Tyler led a party up to the castle, with Abel Ker alongside him. They broke into the jail and freed four of the prisoners chained up in the dungeon. Then, just as their Essex counterparts had done that same day, the Kent rebels turned on the sheriff. They took William Septvantz into their custody and swore him to the same oath that they had imposed upon the mayor and citizens. They demanded that Septvantz hand over all his books containing legal records of the Crown and county and any royal writs in his possession. The collection numbered about fifty in total, and the rebels heaped them in the street in a great public bonfire. To be sure that they had obliterated every piece of royal writing that they could find, they then marched the terrified Septvantz out of town to his manor of Milton, where more writs were kept. These, too, were consigned to the flames.

This, then, was the scene in Canterbury after an entire afternoon of looting and terror: blood ran in the streets, clotting with the fragments of parchment, jagged lumps of broken sealing wax, the ash from bonfires and the charred splinters of destroyed houses. The city and suburbs were in uproar, heaving with insurgent townsmen and aliens from towns and counties miles away. Smoke drifted up from vandalised buildings, blowing out across the Kent downs; and everyone from Canterbury to Dartford quaked at the name of the new pillars of county authority: Wat Tyler and John Ball.

Though the Roman road was in rebel hands, word had still reached London of the chaos in Kent, and on Tuesday, 11 June, royal messengers arrived in Canterbury. They had been sent from the royal court at Windsor, under the authority of the teenage king and his royal council, and they demanded to know why the commons were acting in so monstrous a fashion. They exchanged messages with the rebels throughout the day, and Tyler explained on behalf of his men that they had risen to save the king and the kingdom from traitors, and that they would not desist.

It was a brazen message to send. Clearly the rebels understood the strength of their position – perhaps also they felt they had nothing to lose. Certainly it resonated with the royal council, because by the end of the day, a decision came down from Windsor: Richard sent word that he would meet the rebels in person at Blackheath, on the outskirts of London itself, the next day.

The offer to negotiate with a king was almost too good to believe. Trusting to his lord's good word, and driven by the incredible momentum that had swept his movement along even in its early days, Tyler gathered together his men, organised them for a quick march, and set them out – like pilgrims in reverse – on the greatest mission of all their lives: the advance on London.

PART II

PART II

SIX

BLACKHEATH

The men of Kent and Essex had attracted an army of about one
hundred thousand commons and rustics. They were joined by men
from all parts who were oppressed by debt or feared the censure of
the law because of their misdeeds, and they formed so large a conglomer-
ation of plebeians that no one could remember seeing or hearing of
the like. And so the mob came to the place called 'le Blakheth' where
they decided to view their numbers and count the multitude of their
fellows . . .

THOMAS WALSINGHAM

Blackheath, Wednesday, 12 June

Even with a keen eye and on a clear day, the great south-eastern
point of the Tower of London is not quite visible from the hill at
Greenwich, which juts up in front of Blackheath, into the gentle
countryside close to the banks of the River Thames. But to the tens
of thousands of rebels who gathered on the heath, among the scratchy
dark green undergrowth in the late afternoon of Wednesday, 12 June,
the Tower's presence would have been felt; as imposing and impos-
sibly grand as if they were actually standing before its thick and
heavily fortified walls.

Before them lay the wide maw of the Thames. The best route
along the river was by boat, and on a busy day the Thames – even
this far from the crowded and stinking docks that cut into the City

walls upstream – would have been a noisy, teeming thoroughfare, the powerful tidal waters busy with London's famously foul-mouthed boatmen. Probably the rebels who looked down from the hill saw fewer fishing boats than usual, for the chaos of the last few days had involved a high proportion of men from the Essex fishing villages in the Thames estuary. But the river on Wednesday, 12 June was busy with a different sort of traffic. There had been a flurry of activity all afternoon, with boats bearing messengers between the rebel captains and the king shuttling urgently back and forth through the rough, grey sink.

There had been a steady stream of rebels up to the hill all afternoon – men from Kent and Essex mingling with reinforcements picked up as they moved through the suburban manors and villages that clustered around the capital. It had been known since Tuesday that the men of Kent were coming and the news had infected the villages close to the City with the same sense of agitation that had gripped the shires during the previous fortnight. Right around London's orbit, villages emptied of their excitable inhabitants, all racing to join the excitement taking place along the riverbanks.

As they arrived in their tens of thousands, wild rumours had begun to circulate among the swelling band. As many as sixty thousand people were expected on the hill, with the same number approaching from Essex and Hertfordshire to congregate on the opposite bank of the Thames.[1] It was suggested that the earl of Buckingham was preparing to join the rebel camp. (There were those who said they had seen him in the crowd, and others who said that it was merely a Kentishman who looked like him.) Others passed on a story that Joan of Kent, the queen mother, had bestowed her blessing upon the rebels as she encountered one of the blockades set up on the road from Canterbury, the route along which so many of the rebels had ridden that day. It was a day of high excitement. Legends were already in the making.

Upstream, the royal household had just arrived at the Tower of London. Once agreement to meet Tyler's rebels had been made, the royal court had moved rapidly to leave its sanctuary at Windsor, and had made its way from royal suburbia to the impregnable safety of the City's ancient fortress. In the name of royal security, this was the only practical option.

When the royal train had entered the City, Richard had been met by the mayor, William Walworth, and a trusted group chosen from his closest supporters – men such as Nicholas Brembre, John Philipot and Robert Launde. They had seen him through the City and into the Tower. By evening Richard was embedded among a depleted court that included these Londoners, Treasurer Hales, his half-brother Thomas Holland, the earl of Kent, as well as the earls of Arundel and Warwick, and the earl of Salisbury, a veteran soldier who had fought in France with Richard's father. The court also included 600 courtiers, soldiers and servants.[2] Among these was Richard's cousin, Henry of Derby, and his close friend Robert de Vere, earl of Oxford, both of them teenagers – Derby was not much older than Richard himself, while Oxford was a rather immature nineteen-year-old. The company of contemporaries would have been cold comfort. Richard would have wished for the reassuring presence of Derby's father, John of Gaunt, or their other senior uncle, Edmund Langley, earl of Cambridge.

Unfortunately neither was close. Gaunt, of course, was in Scotland, and Cambridge was in Plymouth, about to set sail with a fleet bound for Portugal. He had been forced to anchor the fleet offshore, for fear of attacks from angry villagers along the south coast. The court also missed the earl of Buckingham, who was occupied at the head of the army in France; Sir Simon Burley, Richard's tutor and a senior knight of the household, was also absent.

Shorn of experience and holed up in a fortress, they faced a situation that was acutely disturbing. When the Tower was built it had been the first great monument to the power of the Norman kings; now it was fast becoming the bolthole of a terrified court, run to ground by its own insurgent people.

If the feeling at court was tense, however, in the rebel camp jubilation reigned. With king and court a mere hour or so upriver, to

Tyler and his followers their liege lord was now tantalisingly close. It was the promise of contact with him which had spurred those who had made the march from Canterbury; and it was the prestige of negotiating with the king himself which bolstered Tyler's position of command. Now, as they waited in the cool of the evening for the next boat to bring word from the Tower, the mere sense that a message was coming directly from the young king himself would have filled the rebel rank-and-file with a combination of foreboding and quasi-religious ecstasy.

Wise to the value of their hostages, Tyler's rebels had maintained in their service Sir John Newton, the keeper of Rochester Castle.[3] Being a knight, he was a useful messenger, so they sent him up to the Tower to announce their arrival. Newton was sent to negotiate the terms of a meeting between king and commons, and although he must have felt the greatest apprehension about his task, after a week in rebel company, no doubt he was glad to go.

As they waited for Newton's return, the rebels decided to make the most of the south bank. By six o'clock in the evening they had announced their presence in Southwark, the town directly adjacent to the bottom end of London Bridge. Southwark was in the hinter-lands of the City, famous for its brothels, prisons and generally unsavoury character. It was an area of colourful ribaldry, where drinkers and pimps rubbed shoulders with cripples, transvestites and whores. The rebels had again, just as in Maidstone, Canterbury and Rochester, engaged in their favourite pastime of jail delivery, ransacking the Marshalsea – where London's prisoners were kept, under the watch of the marshal, Richard Imworth – and removing all the prisoners held there for debt and felony.

The marshal was no hero either to the London citizens or to those in the suburbs. He had had the good sense to flee, earlier in the day, to the City proper. In his absence, the Southwark townsmen rose in partnership with the rebels.

This joint venture between Tyler's rebels, the Southwark mob and the native Londoners opposed to John of Gaunt's policy of using the marshal's office to attempt to bully and control the City was the first open sign that rural and urban rebels were now working in perfectly destructive harmony. (More than likely this was premeditated – during the earlier part of the week, vanguard parties of rebel sympathisers had been passing with relative freedom in and out of the City gates, spreading word of the movement that was building to the south-east.)

At the head of the revolt Wat Tyler, Jack Straw and John Ball must have been filled with a surreal sense both of achievement and of giddy expectation. Ball's philosophy spoke of standing steadfast, true and firm, and of seizing the great moment that God had provided. He would have watched the riots of the ordinary people of England with a feeling that they were a product of divine fate. And he would also have been pleased with a muddled, gloriously inverted time when sins were to be stood on their heads – a time of what he called in his famous sermons 'lechery without shame' and 'gluttony without blame'.

Ball's mystic urgency, backed by the enthusiastic army of thousands that Tyler and regional lieutenants like Ker had mustered, would have created in the leaders' minds a sense that they were about to embark upon the greatest 'summer game' ever played. Looking west along the river with Ball's words in his ear, and then across at his ragtag but determined rank-and-file, Tyler would have felt a great confidence that the game he planned on the grandest scale – to turn London inside out and jest with the king himself – was destined for success.

Before long, out of the river traffic and into the noisy encampment, thick with rumour and expectation, finally came the word that all were waiting for: the royal messenger had arrived.

The king sent word that he would meet the rebels for a conference on the banks of the Thames the next morning. It was a momentous announcement, and vindicated in the rebel minds the purpose and divinity of their mission: to correct the iniquities of the kingdom and demonstrate before their young king the tyranny of his advisers.

That the king had declined to meet that evening, opting rather for the safety of the next morning's light, presented a minor practical problem. With the numbers of rebels camped on Blackheath far exceeding the provisions available, around a quarter of the peasant army were required to spend the night hungry. But it hardly mattered. There was plunder to be had on the south bank for those who could not last until morning. For the rest, food was the last thing on their minds. With the knowledge of the king's agreement to meet them, Tyler and Ball no doubt thought that their position as the scourges of wickedly used authority was about to be given royal blessing.

Unsurprisingly, that excitement translated quickly into further spates of disorder. One of Marshal Imworth's fine Southwark houses had already been torn down, as part of the operation to deliver the Marshalsea; now a series of nightly raids was organised on the houses of all jurors and questmongers (professional legal informers) connected with the marshal. No doubt the names and addresses of these men derived in part from City informers – perhaps the newly freed debtors and felons had their own scores to settle.

Next, the rebels pushed farther along the south bank, to the manor of Lambeth, and stormed the archbishop of Canterbury's palace. They entered the buildings, destroyed Sudbury's goods and burned as many of the archiepiscopal legal records as they could find. They destroyed Sudbury's clothes, vestments and books, and broke open casks of his wine, some of which they drank and some of which they poured scornfully – blasphemously? – on the ground. The force that went to Lambeth must have been sizeable, and their run of the palace total, for they had free enough access to Sudbury's rooms and quarters that they could smash all the kitchen utensils by crashing them together, whooping at their excellent progress as they did so. Their chilling cries as they destroyed the primate's palace – 'A revell! A revell!' – stuck in the minds of clerics throughout London's suburbs.[4] Over the river in Westminister, monks and royal servants must have quaked at the terrible din.

The attack on Sudbury's palace was intended to be symbolic and corrective; the raiding parties returned to Blackheath Hill giddy with success, but not yet overtaken by bloodlust. The monk of Westminster looked back at the revolt and attributed to the rebels even at this early stage the aim of slaughtering Sudbury and all the lawyers in London. But the evidence points to a remarkable discipline among the rebels. Up in Essex, the northern party of the rebels had performed similar rites of destruction on the property and legal records at Cressing Temple, Coggeshall and elsewhere. Unpopular royal officials like John de Bampton and John de Gildesburgh had been threatened, the sheriffs of Essex and Kent kidnapped, and numerous acts of vandalism and housebreaking committed. But even on the worst evenings of orgiastic destruction, there still remained an element of restraint to the rebels' actions. They had, for most of the fortnight of open revolt, largely restricted the focus of their violence to property and records, saving executions for a very few hated enemies. The same held true that night in Southwark. Tyler had his men well marshalled, and they bedded down for the night with negotiation and justice, not bloodletting and murder, on their minds.

So as the chill of a summer night drew in, and the evening of Wednesday, 12 June turned into the early hours of Thursday 13th – the festival of Corpus Christi – the crackle and glow of campfires would have lined the heath, casting an eerie, wavering light over excited, dirty faces, filled with pride and expectation. An incredible adventure was about to reach its climax before the highest, most worshipful authority of all. The fires may just have appeared as tiny orange pinpricks in the night, visible from the Tower upriver, where a young king slept, preparing for the first great showdown of his life.

SEVEN

THE TRUE COMMONS

The king had his barges got ready and . . . travelled to Greenwich. But there the Chancellor and Treasurer informed the king that it would be too great folly to go to the commons for they were unreasonable men and did not know how to behave . . . And the said commons had a watch-word in English among themselves, 'With whom haldes yow?', to which the reply was, 'Wyth kynge Richarde and with the trew communes' . . .

Anonimalle Chronicle

London, Thursday, 13 June (Corpus Christi)

The sound of London's church bells ringing on Corpus Christi had, since the turn of the century, marked the beginning of a day of boisterous popular piety. It was a feast day given over specifically to honour the wonder of the Eucharist, in which thin slivers of unleavened bread and viscous droplets of wine were transformed into the body and blood of Jesus Christ. A relatively new festival, it had been established in Europe since the mid-thirteenth century, but quickly gained wide popularity as a time to celebrate not only the most miraculous sacrament of the Church, but one that also had profound social significance.

London's trade guilds loved Corpus Christi. It was a time to display their wealth, numbers and superiority over rivals as a day of parades and church processions spread throughout the City, spilling from the churches into the taverns, and from the taverns back into the streets.

It was self-consciously a summer feast, in which the streets of towns were strewn with rushes and garlanded with flags, and in which the whole community (and smaller tight-knit groups within it) turned out as one to celebrate their unity, bound together by the remembrance and return of Christ's broken body. Corpus Christi was characterised by noise and colour, and an organised shirking of the shackles.[1]

Corpus Christi in 1381 bore with it all these things and more. The City was buzzing, both inside and out, with an unprecedented number of strangers. Within the walls there were already many visitors from Essex and Kent, who had been agitating all week. They would have brought news of the disturbances in the countryside and traded speculation about what was to come in the days ahead. Outside the walls, two distinct parties were organising. The band of Essex companies that had been tilting at houses belonging to royal officials and hunting their terrified servants for the last ten days were now camped in the fields near Mile End, a few miles up the Aldgate Road, a road whose entrance to the City was just 1500 yards north of the Tower. They must have known full well that there were Kent rebels amassed downriver in Greenwich, camped on Blackheath Hill, carrying out their own assaults on Southwark and Lambeth.

Inside the Tower, King Richard and his court were rising and preparing to face the most testing day of the short reign. The rebels that had approached from the south-east were now camped virtually on their doorstep. As well as Tyler's followers, in Blackheath, parties of rebels from Essex would have begun arriving at the north-east gates of the City. The royal servant and poet Geoffrey Chaucer, who rented an apartment above the Aldgate, could well have looked out of his window and spotted groups of Essex men milling around below, having wandered down the road from their own base camp at Mile End. It was as clear to those waking in the Tower as it was to the rebels camped in the open air that this Corpus Christi day had the potential to be extremely explosive.

The most immediate problem facing the court was a fresh crisis of leadership. Overnight Richard had received an unwelcome and highly disturbing visit from Simon Sudbury, the archbishop of Canterbury, who had come to him and resigned the Great Seal, the symbol of his chancellorship. Sudbury had been forced to flee from Lambeth as the rebels approached. This shock, together with the savage violence that had torn through his diocesan seat at Canterbury, had contrived to shred the ageing archbishop's nerves. He may have blamed himself for the disastrous decision to levy the Northampton tax that had stirred the commons into their present state of ungodly uproar. His resignation was no doubt considered; but it was also cowardly. Sudbury had been a part of Richard's life since he was a small boy – now he was abandoning his fourteen-year-old king as catastrophe loomed.

As he prepared for the mass that would have marked the beginning of the observances of the holy feast day and contemplated the presentation to the rebel bands later that morning, Richard may have been reminded of an earlier occasion of public display. At his coronation, when he was aged just ten, he had been paraded aloft on his tutor Simon Burley's shoulders through the adoring throngs at Westminster, and hailed in the streets with extraordinary displays of fealty and pageantry. Sudbury, then, had appeared in all his archiepiscopal glory to anoint Richard with holy oils, and crown him as king. Sudbury, then gentle, wise, paternal and pious, invested him as semidivine, a young demigod among fully grown men. As Richard received the sword of office, Sudbury had told him to use it to 'execrate and destroy those of the faith who are false', and to 'glory in the triumph of good and as a great minister of justice be worthy to rule eternally with the Saviour of the world'. And after Richard was invested with the sceptre – the symbol of royal power – Sudbury had told him to use it to 'correct the sinful, give peace to the righteous and give your aid in directing them to continue in the right way, so that after ruling in your earthly kingdom you may attain to the eternal kingdom'.[2]

In this time of popular crisis, it is quite probable that these sentiments and phrases would have come to Richard's mind. He stepped out of mass (probably held in the Tower chapel of St Peter ad Vincula – appropriately, St Peter in Chains) down the thin steps to the fortress's landing jetty and on to the royal barge, accompanied by his defeated former Chancellor. Hales joined them, as did Warwick and Salisbury.

A party of royal knights followed, and a selection from the beleaguered court brought up the rear in a train of four more barges. The
lead boat pushed off into the Thames – leaving behind a City in noisy
preparation for a particularly raucous day of festivities – and pressed
downriver towards a people in dire need of royal correction.

Expectation of the king's barge had been feverish on Blackheath
Hill, and the deputation that was detached to negotiate with the king's
party on the banks of the river at the royal manor of Rotherhithe
was enormous. Perhaps more than one tenth of the entire Kent rebel
army rode and marched behind Tyler, many of them in a heightened
state of agitation owing to the auspicious occasion, the festive overtures of Corpus Christi, and a night spent outdoors on an empty
stomach. They brought with them their two flags of St George and
a decent number of their sixty pennons – rectangular flags with a
V-shape cut into them, which were used in conventional military
formations to denote separate companies of soldiers. Tyler was a
competent general, and would have wanted his men carefully ranked
and kept to order in expectation of his grandest moment.

So the rebels waited. But they did not wait peacefully. Corpus
Christi was Ball's day, and straining against the good order demanded
by a meeting with the king was a wild, righteous zeal, which the
preacher whipped up in the rebels' hearts early that morning in one
of the greatest sermons of his life. He had taken as his theme a familiar
rhyming proverb that struck at the very heart of all who heard it:

> When Adam delved and Eve span,
> Who, then, was the gentleman?

This sort of radical egalitarian theme was a mainstay of popular
preaching, and had earned Ball much favour with the disenfranchised
and poor. It was also what made him such a dangerous heretic to the
Church hierarchy, compounding as he did both heresy and sedition
in an easy couplet that would trip off the lips of even the rudest parish-
ioner. To the authorities, his proverb was gross and blasphemous,
rejecting wholesale a human hierarchy that to conventional minds was

divinely ordained and instituted. It was also a pointed attack on the ease and luxury of the landed political classes, who neither delved nor spun, and in doing so dodged God's punishment, issued at the Fall, when man was cursed to labour for his survival.[3] But to his audience, inclined more than at any time in their lives to loathe the corruptions and ill-used ease of their social betters, it was music to the ears.

Ball preached that morning on the nature of human equality – that in the beginning there had been no division between men, and that God had never ordained such an unfair institution as serfdom:

> Ah, ye good people, the matters goeth not well to pass in England, nor shall do till everything be commons, and that there be no villains nor gentlemen, but that we may be all united together, and that the lords be no greater masters than we![4]

Heads would have nodded among his audience, and cries of approval would have greeted him when he thundered that now was the time to cast aside the yoke of servitude and serfdom, and to enjoy the liberty that each of his flock yearned for:

> What have we deserved, or why should we thus be kept in servage? We be all come from one father and one mother, Adam and Eve: whereby can they say or show that they be greater lords than we be, saving by that they cause us to win and labour for that they dispend?
>
> They are clothed in velvet and camlet furred with grise, and we be vestured with poor cloth: they have their wines, spices and good bread, and we have the drawing out of the chaff and drink water: they dwell in fair houses, and we have the pain and travail, rain and wind in the fields; and by that that cometh of our labours they keep and maintain their estates: we be called their bondsmen and without we do readily them service, we be beaten; and we have no sovereign to whom we may complain, nor that will hear us nor do us right.

Never mind that Kent was, in fact, one of the few English counties in which there was no serfdom left; in the county where the lower orders had tasted freedom and legal liberty in morsels but never in its entirety, this was, of course, an even more powerful appeal to the heart. The crowd could hardly ask for more.

Ball had likened his vision of the promised land they were all on the brink of achieving to a field, in which the good husbandmen should now get rid of the weeds that threatened to choke the wheat – those weeds, he said, were the great lords of the realm; the lawyers and justices and jurors, as well as any who did not share his vision of a free and equal society.

On Corpus Christi, this would have resonated in the hearts of his listeners, their minds filled with images of Christ the ploughman, bearing his cross like the wooden handle of the plough. Ball conjured a powerful, mystical righteousness in the hearts of his audience, and showed them a promised land, in which England's order was not stood on its head, but reformed and cleansed of the inequities of power. He promised peace and security, and proclaimed that this day of Corpus Christi was about to present them with the opportunity to carry out a divine cull of society – a cull that at any moment would be started with the arrival of the king.

Rotherhithe was a little farther upstream than Blackheath, and the rebel party would have been able to see the royal barge train almost as soon as it left the Tower. They would have seen the rich colours of the splendidly adorned lead barge catch the light, their hearts hanging on the tantalising pull of the little oars through the grey water of the Thames: their king inching towards them, silent and magnificent.

In the midst of the crowd, Sir John Newton, still a rebel hostage, would have felt a wall of noise building, as the barge crept around the river's right-hand bend and ever closer into view. He might have seen Tyler, Ball and Straw, together at the head of their band, visibly steeling themselves for the sight of their life: the quasi-divine king – still little more than a child, but anointed and glorious, and here just for them.

Newton would also have tried to imagine the tension aboard the barge. He had been exposed to, and understood, the rebels' rough, loud methods. Richard had not yet clapped eyes on them. In his report to the court the previous day Newton had been instructed to assure the king that the rebels meant him no harm; but with the whooping and hollering that were building around the mob, Richard was going to be hard pressed to believe him.

Indeed, the barge's passengers were growing steadily more nervous. The closer the vast and fevered host on the shore appeared, the greater was the concern for Richard's physical safety. Sudbury, sitting alongside the king, was still gripped with the panic of the night. As they drew nearer and the rebels' halloos grew ever louder and more urgent, he may have been able to pick out Newton, terrified still for his life in the midst of the fray.

The fright that hung over Sudbury had also infected Hales. He, too, had had his house wrecked at the rebels' hands and was acutely aware that even if the king were to be welcomed by the rebels, he, as treasurer, Essex landowner and prior of the Knights Hospitallers, was most definitely not. He began to caution against negotiation with such a frightening crowd of bare-legged rascals. The ill ease spread. Salisbury, as chief soldier on the barge, also weighed against landing near such a dangerous-looking and, by his standards, ill-disciplined army. That they were roughly armed with rusty swords and old bows only made them appear more unpredictable. There were no known rules of engagement for an army of rustics led by their own kind – normally these were the rabble put out for slaughter under foreign nobles.

Dissuaded from any thoughts of youthful boldness by the counsel of these three older men – all of whom were at least thirty-five years his senior – Richard abandoned all thoughts of going ashore. The safest option was to remain on the water, so rather than landing Richard consented to receive a petition from the rebels.

Word went across the water to Tyler's men, and without delay a written schedule of demands was brought out to the royal barge by a yeoman. Its contents were shocking. Stirred up by Ball's flamboyant sermon that morning, and dizzy with their own success, the rebels sent a petition that required not subtle forms of political restitution, or legal redress, but the crude justice of heads on poles. They demanded the death of all around the king whom they thought guilty of perverting the realm. They included John of Gaunt, Sudbury, Hales, Bishop Courtenay of London, Bishop Fordham of Durham, who was Clerk of the Privy Seal, the Chief Justice, Sir Robert Belknap, Sir Ralph Ferrers (the knight Gaunt protected for his infamous part in the Hawley affair in 1378), Sir Robert Plessington, Chief Baron of the Exchequer, John Legge, the serjeant-at-arms popularly associated with farming out the poll tax inquiry commissions, and John de Bampton, the egregious Brentwood tax collector himself.

The council on the river was stunned. Although the king protested his willingness to address the raucous, hotchpotch army of his people, he was overruled. Unsurprisingly, with two of the targets of this gruesome petition on the barge itself, any thin, lingering prospect of going anywhere near the baying mob on the south bank now evaporated. The rebels' watchword, 'With whom holds you?' – answerable by 'With King Richard and the true commons' – was in their minds a clear badge of loyalty. But it meant nothing to Sudbury and Hales. To them, the only safe action, and that which the royal party took without a moment's ado, was to bolt for the security of the Tower. They sent word to the rebels that if they wished to continue negotiations, they might do so at Windsor the following Monday. The barges turned in the water and began to move once more upstream towards the City.

On the shores there was disbelief. Tyler's army stood on the river-banks, their climactic moment now ebbing way. The hurrahs and bellows of exultation turned into howls of anguish, screams of rage and denial, and a furious impulse to action. Livid at the snub during what should have been their moment of greatest triumph, the leadership turned their inflamed party around and set off back to Blackheath Hill. Restraint was ebbing away, leaving behind it a raw plane of retributive fury. The moratorium was over. London Bridge stood a couple of hours' march away; the party of Essex rebels at the brink of the Aldgate. Against the will of the true commons, there could be no escape for traitors to the realm. A Corpus Christi parade unlike any seen before was about to descend upon the City, and the wicked were to be plucked from the ground, like so many wretched weeds.

EIGHT

THE BRIDGE

> The slavish band, which utter lunacy possessed, tried to join the hand
> of victory with theirs. And so the savage throngs approached the city
> like the waves of the sea and entered it by violence.
>
> JOHN GOWER

Southwark, Thursday, 13 June 1381

The mob stood, stunned. Then their anger, whipped up by their
leaders, burst out. When Gower remembered the days at
Blackheath, it was Ball and Tyler's rabble-rousing which dominated
his description:

> The whole mob was silent and took note of the speaker's words, and
> they liked every command he delivered from his mouth. The rabble
> lent a deluded ear to his fickle talk, and it saw none of the future things
> that would result . . . so the Jackdaw [Tyler] stirred up all the others
> with his outrageous shouting, and he drew the people's minds toward
> war . . . He said, 'Strike,' and one man struck. He said, 'Kill,' and another
> killed. He said, 'commit crime'; everyone committed it, and did not
> oppose his will . . .[1]

The primal fury that Gower recalled had possessed Tyler, Straw,
Ball and the rest of the rebel leadership since their snub by the royal
party earlier that morning. As they had begun to move from

Blackheath, the plans they laid became tinged with indignant fantasy. After the revolt, Straw was said to have confessed that the rebels plotted not merely to confront the king, but to capture him and parade him around the country as a figurehead for John Ball's vision of destroying all forms of noble and ecclesiastical hierarchy.

If these plans existed they were a knee-jerk response to the impotence the rebels felt in their moment of highest expectation. As they moved west along the Thames from Blackheath towards Southwark, their mood grew dark, and their desire to release the pent-up tension that had built all through the night had reached a new intensity. The City of London was now a fortress to be stormed.

Of course, storming a fortress required the right combination of guile and brute force. The main obstacle to entering London was the river. There was only one bridge across the Thames – London Bridge, which straddled the water between Southwark on the south bank and the church of St Magnus at Bridge Street, just a few hundred yards west of the smelly clutter of Billingsgate fish market. The bridge was a great commercial highway built in stone, with shops along its whole length and a stone chapel in the centre. Towards the Southwark end was a great drawbridge, and it was this which secured the City against invasion. There was no way that Tyler could hope to get his men across the Thames' powerful tidal waters solely by boat. Somehow they would have to secure a passage across the bridge.

In this respect they had the advantage of good contacts within the City. It was no secret that there were many among the lower ranks who wished to see the rebels come to town. But there were also a few sympathisers in the upper reaches of City society. The most prominent of these was Alderman John Horn. (After the revolt, five aldermen – Horn, Adam Carlisle, Walter Sybil, William Tongue and John Fresh – were all accused of being to some degree in league with the rebels, but in all cases except that of Horn, this seems unlikely.[2]) Horn had met the rebels the previous day at Blackheath as part of the process of negotiation that had been under way between the rebels and the royal and municipal authorities. He had actually been sent by Mayor Walworth with a sharp warning to the rebels not to enter the City. But Horn did not relay the message with anything like its due conviction, and the rebels seem to have gathered from his demeanour that there were those close to the summit of power in London who were sympathetic to their cause.

There was, of course, definitely sympathy for the rebels among the common folk of the City, who realised that there was a broad community of interests between Tyler's men and themselves. Hatred of and opposition to John of Gaunt stood at the head of the list of shared grievances. That Gaunt was far away from London mattered little – he had property in and around London, ripe to feed an increasingly agitated populace's appetite for destruction.

The thirst for a reckoning was contagious, and it is likely that on Corpus Christi there was an especially heightened sense of community among the marching guilds turning out into the streets for the festival, and the organised band of peasants on the other side of the river. For their superiors in City government, there was also the worry about what the Essex rebels, who had only a gate to contend with, and those rebels already inside the City, might exact in retribution if they were to enter the City and find their Kentish comrades thwarted.

There was also the matter of Southwark itself. It had been infected by the same spirit of chaos that had gripped the rest of London's suburbs, and was ready to rise both from within and without. As the bands of Kent rebels approached – their numbers swelling with Southwark natives – they made for a brothel tucked away on the banks of the Southwark fishponds in a house rented from Mayor Walworth. They tore it down and set fire to it, terrifying the Flemish prostitutes inside, and delighting those in the City proper who disapproved of the squalid tenement. Agile and angry, the rebels demonstrated their tenacity by scrambling on to rooftops and smashing buildings to the ground. The loyal people of Southwark who remained cried to the citizens on the north bank of the Thames that Southwark would not survive much more of an onslaught.[3]

There followed a short stand-off, as the rebels stood on the southern third of London Bridge, and a mob of excited Londoners looked back at them from the north, watching plumes of smoke curl upwards from Walworth's smouldering whorehouse. Looking past the raised drawbridge, Tyler's men would have seen Walworth himself, the inscrutable fishmonger, politician, financier and courtier, nominally in charge of the City but probably aware that he was past the point of resisting the tide of public will. Walworth surely realised that he did not command, in the City militia, anything like the resources to disperse them or to control the City, especially if rebellion spread and took root among the Londoners themselves. The rebels' most inspired move had been to make it publicly known that they did not approach London with the intention of plundering; that they would buy provisions at market prices; and that the people of the City need not fear the destruction of their property. They were on the hunt for traitors.

In the light of all this, Walworth realised that resistance was no longer an option. As the welcoming swell grew, with a resigned nod from the leaders of Bridge Ward, under whose immediate jurisdiction London Bridge fell, the bridge's keeper let down the drawbridge, and the Kentishmen, seeing their path stretch out before them, flooded into London. Announcing themselves with a cacophony of diabolical howls, they swept forward past the little shops and the buildings that leaned hugger-mugger about the Chapel of St Thomas à Becket in the middle of the bridge, towards the Church of St Magnus on the riverbank. Beneath their feet, the powerful water of the Thames rushed hard, swirling in dangerous eddies through the bridge's tight arches. Seven hundred yards past Billingsgate to the east, the Tower stood impregnable but now open to close siege; upriver, past the commercial docks on either side of the ancient corn port of Queenhithe, the mouth of the River Fleet marked the western boundary of the City, where the busy commercial riverbanks gave way to luxurious palace wharfs and the rolling gardens and orchards that belonged to the bishops' palaces. Straight ahead lay the close, dirty streets of England's capital, thick with excitable, drunken rascals and wealthy traders alike, the timid scuttling for cover, and all the clergy of the city rushing away to pray for peace in a time of chaos.[4]

Ahead of the incoming rural rebels, the City mob gathered and set out with a single common purpose for the western gates of London's wall. Beyond the huge wooden roof of the Norman cathedral of St Paul's lay the Ludgate, a stone entrance to the City rebuilt and fortified the previous century with stones removed from the houses of London's rich Jews, and decorated with statues of England's ancient monarchs, including King Lud, the pre-Christian King of the British. The gate opened into Fleet Street, which in turn became the Strand. These were the main streets of medieval suburbia, the green-acred outskirts of the City, dotted with gated palaces and gardens backing on to the Thames – its pleasant and clean atmosphere a far cry from the cramped, dirty streets of the City. Interspersed between the residences were around fifty goldsmiths, selling silver salt cellars, drinking cups and finger bowls, along with plenty of popular pewter plates. The Londoners piled through the Ludgate and into this well-to-do neighbourhood.

There was one residence along the Strand that stood aloft from all the others: John of Gaunt's great Savoy Palace. As befitted the richest man in England, it was a masterpiece of architecture and luxury; Gaunt's military expeditions had allowed him to take to a new level the already impressive splendour of a residence that had served the dukes of Lancaster since Edmund Crouchback, the first earl, had lived there in the previous century.

The Kent rebels ran behind the Londoners. The Savoy was on their list of targets, but geographically they had other, more immediate concerns: the jails. By freeing prisoners they were making a pointed stand against the power of the law. It also provided an opportunity to increase their numbers with men who might be relied upon to put their experience of causing trouble to good use.

As they headed for the first jail on their list of targets, Tyler's men held their discipline and made their way through the south-west quarter of the City without succumbing to an urge to loot or to terrorise the general population. Instead, they too flooded through the narrow streets to the Ludgate. Having left the City's walls almost as rapidly as they entered them, the rebels turned right up the banks of the Fleet river, and stormed towards the Fleet prison. They broke into the prison and freed everyone who was held there – many of whom were debtors, a class of prisoner for whom the Fleet had earned a reputation as early as 1290. As with the Marshalsea, the purpose was an attack on the law and abuses of the law in general – any concern about letting genuine malefactors back into the community was completely disregarded.

The Kentishmen's ranks were now swollen by another arrival, for in the east of the City, the Aldgate had finally been opened to the Essex rebels. Influenced by the likes of Thomas Farringdon and the London butcher Adam atte Welle they had either persuaded or coerced the gatekeepers into letting them into the City. For the City's guardians to have thought of holding out after the bridge had fallen would have been suicidal. The Essex men rushed in to join the charge being led by the London rebels and the radical Kent wing about whom they had heard so much during the previous fortnight.

With native Londoners for their guides, the Essex rebels' path through the City was assured. And when they, too, flooded out of the Ludgate, past the stony gaze of the famous British kings who decorated it, and joined their Kentish comrades in a jubilant march down the paved streets of suburbia, west towards the Savoy, their hearts would have been filled with jubilant, reforming fire. They bellowed into the afternoon sun and waved their swords and axes in the air, drunk on success and ready to tear the duke of Lancaster's proud palace to the ground.

NINE

FIRST FLAMES

And at last they came before the Savoy, broke open the gates, entered
the place and came to the wardrobe. They took all the torches they
could find, and lighted them, and burnt all the cloths, coverlets and
beds, as well as all the very valuable head-boards . . . All the napery
and other goods they could discover they carried into the hall and
set on fire with their torches . . . They burnt the hall and the chambers as well as all the apartments within the gates . . . and the commons
of Kent received the blame for this arson, but some said that the
Londoners were really guilty of this deed . . .

Anonimalle Chronicle

London, Thursday, 13 June, 3 p.m.
Any stragglers in the band that hurtled down the hill out of Ludgate
and past the sprung gates of the Fleet prison to their right would have
seen before them an orgy of destruction already in full flow. The heat
of the afternoon sun was just beginning to mellow, but the fury of the
rebels' retribution on their enemies was edging towards blistering point.

Outside London's walls, but inside the City boundary, which was
marked by a series of bars hammered into the ground in a jagged semi-
circle around London's periphery, there were several large plots of land
occupied by the wealthy and well-to-do. Both the Carmelites (or White
Friars) and the bishop of Salisbury, whose pleasant riverside dwellings
were ordinarily among the first to be encountered by a visitor strolling

along Fleet Street, would have echoed to the sound of the rushing feet and raucous voices of the rebels as they pounded out of the City they had only recently broken into. Fear gripped the holy orders in particular – they had suffered disproportionately throughout England during the course of the revolt. But the friars and the bishop's men need not have worried, for the rebels were quite focused on specific targets, and they were not in the main motivated by anticlericalism.

These targets included, for a start, any house belonging to Marshal Imworth, of which there were several on the fringes of the City. As these were pointed out, rebels leapt up to rip off the roofs and set fire to the buildings beneath. The marshal himself, understanding that his unhealthily close connection with Gaunt – and his office's symbolic attachment with tyrannical and unjust authority – was enough to mark him out as a hunted man, had gone into hiding. He feared the worst, following the debacle of the previous day, in which his official and private possessions in Southwark had been comprehensively trashed.

After Whitefriars and the bishop of Salisbury's Inn, the first really great dwelling along the road was the New Temple. Originally the grand dwelling place of the Knights Templar in the twelfth century, for the past seventy-three years it had been in the possession of their rivals, the Knights Hospitaller, of whom Treasurer Hales was the prior. The Temple was leased by the Hospitaller to London's lawyers and provided lodgings for legal trainees and a repository for important legal documents and records. As the spiritual home of the legal profession, and a place crammed with the documents and charters that they despised, it was a building with a special significance to the rebels, who reserved the same sort of venom for lawyers and practitioners – or, as they saw them, corruptors – of the law as they did for politicians such as Hales.

The rebels burst into the Temple grounds, and began to tear down the lodging houses and buildings that occupied six or seven acres of prime, beautiful land stretching down to the Thames. Men clambered on to the rooftops and (ironically, given their commander) threw down the tiles until the roofs were in a bare and pitiful state. Next, the rebels forced their way into the Temple's round church. This stunning building had been copied from the Holy Sepulchre at Jerusalem, with the sharply projecting porch that characterised the original; the rebels marched in though this and found their way to the treasure house, where the most valuable books, rolls and remembrances were kept.[1] These were the highest badges of a legal system that in rebel eyes preferred contracts and statutes to trusted community tradition, and the rebels plundered the trove with glee. They squeezed back out of the narrow porch, their arms laden with enrolled parchment, which they took up to the high road, gathered into a large pile and burned. It was a damning funeral pyre for England's legal system, and the road would once more have filled with yelps and whoops of pleasure.

This was not base vandalism. It was a pointed attack on a legal profession that the rebels hated for squashing and oppressing them, for using chicanery and book learning to damage their condition, and for putting unjust rules in place where natural justice ought to have prevailed. Their revenge was crude, but it was horribly effective.

The sack of the Temple prompted a more general letting-off of steam among the rebels, who had held off from general vandalism throughout the entry into London. The reins were loosened a little, and smaller bands of rebels ran up and down the road, pulling down the houses of questmongers (professional legal informers) and setting fire to anything they could not destroy with their hands.

With the Temple records and the lawmakers' houses fuelling fires along the road, and the hour of the afternoon creeping round towards four o'clock, the rebels moved on to the main prize – the Savoy.[2]

Passing between the bars of the City, and into suburbia proper, the crowd continued along Fleet Street until it became the Strand. On the left they passed the great succession of Bishops' Inns – Exeter, Bath, Llandaff, Coventry and Worcester – the Church of St Mary le Strand, and a string of smaller shops and houses. All of these buildings and grand ecclesiastical mansions were in fact part of the duchy of Lancaster, and therefore in some way connected with John of Gaunt; but none held the special appeal to the rebels of the palace of Savoy itself. They plundered a few tuns of wine from one of the bishops' cellars but otherwise saved their energies for the duke's house.

When they arrived there, the rural bands found that some keener Londoners – who saw Gaunt as their special enemy above all others – had been at the palace for some time. So as new waves of Essex and Kent men rolled in, they would have been greeted by an almighty clamour and, already, the first wisps of smoke curling up into the summer afternoon sky.

For those rebels who had never seen the Savoy before, the vast, opulent expanse of it would have taken their breath away. It was known with good reason as the finest palace in England, and had cost around £35,000 to build – the equivalent of around four and a half months' wages for an entire English army. Gaunt's father-in-law had funded its construction with wealth plundered during the high point of the Hundred Years War. Huge walls barricaded its grounds from the Strand. Within lay a multitude of buildings – the state apartments, the great hall, a private chapel, cloisters, a few meaner, thatched buildings and stables, and a fishpond. Gates opened out on to the Strand on the north side, and to the Thames in the south, where, as with all riverside mansions, a jetty allowed the duke and his servants to travel back and forth between the City, Westminster and Sheen by water.

Now all these splendid buildings were surrounded by chaos. The Strand-side gates were broken, and rebels ran freely between the high road and the palatial gardens. Those servants who had remained in the palace while Gaunt was in the north on his diplomatic mission had scattered, either along the river or down the road towards the village of Charing, taking with them what they could: a bed and a handful of other items. Everything left was condemned. The rebels who arrived shortly after showed no mercy: furniture, tapestries and all manner of possessions were piled up in huge bonfires in the street. Any torch that could be found was grabbed and used to burn the mansion's cloths, coverlets and beds. The duke's 1000-mark decorated headboard was burnt, as was his table linen, which was carried to the great hall and built into another fire. From this petty arson, the hall itself caught light. The fire was then deliberately spread to the chambers and apartments of the manor.

Meanwhile, below the main rooms of the palace, a group of thirty or so rebels came across the duke's wine cellar. Throughout all the raids, the rebels had adhered to a strict code, true to the compact made between the Londoners and the Kent men: there was to be no looting of goods, only the destruction of ill-gotten wealth, corrupt lawyers and traitors. Nevertheless, a jovial little party broke out as the cases and kegs of Gaunt's sweet wine were burst open. As the wine flowed there was much singing, joking around and marvelling at the fine new circumstances in which the group found themselves.

Above them, as the rebels and the Londoners continued to pull apart the duke's magnificent palace, greater and greater discoveries were made. Barrels of gold and silver plate were turned up. Some were dragged up to the roadside and smashed, and others rolled down to the riverside gates and hurled into the Thames. Jewels were stamped on and crushed into dust to ensure they could not be rescued or reused. Gilded cups were beaten out of shape by rebels wielding swords and axes. That which could not be adequately mangled or smelted on the bonfires was thrown into the sewers. As the excitement built, some of the mob began to pocket Gaunt's wealth for themselves: one small party loaded an ornate chest worth £1000 into a boat and removed it to Southwark, where they divided up the spoils between them. But this sort of behaviour was soon stamped out, when another rebel was spotted trying to hide a silver goblet from the duke's wardrobe in his pocket. He was grabbed and hurled into the flames for violating Tyler's strict instructions not to turn a symbolic event into a thieves' paradise. As the pilferer burned to death, a stark warning was issued to the rest of the crowd – anyone else caught stealing would suffer the same fate.

As the screams of the condemned man rang out above the roar of the burning palace, there was a sudden explosion. Fire had already been spreading through the timbers and walls of the palace, weakening its structure and making it an ever more risky task for the rest of the rebels to remove the duke's goods. Now, to make it worse, three barrels presumed to contain gold or silver had been hurled into the furnace in the hall. They had, in fact, contained gunpowder, and the blaze erupted. Before long, a section of the building collapsed.

Timber crumpled and stone crashed downwards, causing a huge blockade of the wine cellars and completely trapping the thirty revellers inside. They began to cry out, but above the noise and the excitement outside, no one could hear them.

In a final act of humiliation for the absent Gaunt, one of his fine vestments was brought into the street. The contemporary term was a 'jakke' – a padded and richly embroidered jerkin. It was hoisted above the crowd on the end of a lance, and all those rebels with bows and arrows took the opportunity for target practice. They loosed off flurries of arrows, which thudded into the padding, ruining the rich and expensive garment. When it had been riddled enough, the lance was lowered, and the mob tore the trophy to bits with their weapons. It was not the duke himself, but it was a cathartic substitute.

With gunpowder aiding its demise, the Savoy now became more of a spectacle than a sport, and the rebels began to split into bands. One band charged off down the road towards Charing and Westminster, where they carried out another jailbreak at Westminster jail. By this stage, word seems to have reached those invested with any sort of royal or municipal authority that resistance was futile. After delivering Westminster, the party took a long loop back up from village suburbia to rejoin the fray at Newgate, a few hundred yards up the City wall from Ludgate. Here there was yet another prison break taking place, as Newgate jail was delivered of its inhabitants, and another set of vagabonds, felons and debtors was released from the filthy riverside dungeon, back through the Newgate itself and into the City's mutinous throng.

As evening drew in, the fires along the Strand raged on, sending out great plumes of smoke that were visible right across the City, sparks lighting up the gloaming and wisps of soot and ash carrying in the cooling summer air. In the cellar of the Savoy, thirty frightened revellers continued to batter and scream at the debris that kept them trapped underground, surrounded by wine, but no longer celebrating. Passers-by heard them, but no one dared, or cared, to help. The next morning the cries continued; after seven days of neglect, whether suffocated or starved, they were no more.

TEN

UNDER SIEGE

Afterwards they came to the beautiful priory of the [Hospital of St John, Clerkenwell] and set on fire several fine and pleasant buildings within it – a great and horrible piece of damage to the priory for all time to come ... At this time the king was in a turret of the great Tower of London, and saw the manor of the Savoy and the Hospital of Clerkenwell ... all in flames. He called all the lords about him in to a chamber and asked their counsel as to what should be done in such a crisis. But none of them could or would give him any counsel ...

Anonimalle Chronicle

London, Thursday, 13 June, 6 p.m.
Roger Legett was an assizer, a questmonger, a professional lawyer and, by popular consensus, a rogue. He had made a successful career in London mainly by demonstrating total moral flexibility in return for cash payment. The law had made him extremely wealthy, and he had built up a fine collection of lands and property around the western suburbs of the City. The law had also made him many enemies, not least among those who knew he had spent two years in the Fleet prison during the 1370s for putting vicious mantraps in the ditches around his land. Now, trembling inside the Collegiate Church of St Martin-le-Grand in the early evening, he guessed that his time was finally up.[1]

By the later hours of the afternoon, the rebel mob had splintered

97

into groups about the City – still organised by company and just about holding to the principle of dispensing justice, rather than looting and pillaging, but no longer held together en masse quite so firmly as they had been when they were first outside the City walls. The great popular triumph of the day so far had been the burning of the Savoy, but around that had begun to revolve bodies of smaller, pettier, more private acts of retribution. The commoners of London had joined enthusiastically with the rural rebels, and the heterogeneous mob's many and varied purposes formed an emulsion of private feuds and pursuits of individual justice within the fluid swell of the broader revolt.[2]

It would have been hard to find a man in all of London on that Thursday who was brave enough to defend Legett against the bands that sought him. In the rebels' eyes, he stood for everything that was treacherous – for years he had profited from dispensing partial justice and conniving with colleagues like the undersheriff of London John Butterwick to obstruct, delay or deny due process of law and, therefore, the true and dutiful governance of England. He showed little concern for the life or limb of those who crossed him.

Now it was payback time. That afternoon Legett had made a will, evacuated his house and fled for the safety of St Martin-le-Grand. It was hardly an inspired hiding place, for this royal free chapel, with its right of permanent sanctuary, was well known as the bolthole of every rascal and fugitive in London. It was dedicated to the fourth-century bishop of Tours who had made his name by giving half of his cloak to a beggar, and those who ran there did so in the expectation of ecclesiastical protection – on the tacit understanding that no one who feared the wrath of God and the Church would dare breach sanctuary.

Unfortunately for Legett, the rebel band who found him felt that the weight of divine favour on that day rested with them, and not with the canons of St Martin's. A group of them barged into the chapel and found Legett clinging to the high altar. They took him prisoner, and marched him out into the thronging street.

Leggett was dragged from St Martin's, down the road known as

West Cheap to Cheapside, a popular intersection of roads in the heart of the walled City. If he craned his head over his right shoulder as he was bundled through the streets, he would have seen the gigantic spire of St Paul's cathedral, towering some 450 feet into the evening sky, and casting its long shadow east over the troubled City.

When the gang carrying him reached Cheapside, at the confluence of Milk Street, Wood Street and Bread Street, they stopped. This was a well-known place of trade, conversation, preaching, water-gathering and public punishment. Legett was pushed to the ground, the crowd all around eager to see justice done against one who had for so long perverted it. If Legett had kept his eyes open, his last sight may have been the Eleanor Cross that stood in the open street, its four hexagonal steps leading up to six idealised statues of the beloved queen. The cross was one of twelve laid by Eleanor's grieving husband, Edward I, to mark the twelve stages of her body's progress from Lincoln to its final resting place in Westminster Abbey. Legett may, amid the clamour and the bloodlust, have thought of the will he had written that afternoon, which asked his own wife, Emma, to do with his body 'what God shall will'. Or perhaps fear and the awful proximity of death blocked everything from his mind. Soon the axe fell, tearing his head from his body, his neck pumping warm, sticky blood on to the Cheap.

Legett's was one of eighteen heads to roll that evening, as the City grew frenzied with the urge for retribution. Just outside the City walls, meanwhile, a larger band of rebels was following the Holborn river north towards Clerkenwell. This was another varied troupe, with rural and urban rebels rubbing shoulders for the mile or so's hike due north. Among them were artisans, servants, apprentices, farmers and traders. There was even a falconer in the service of the prior himself among the rabble; and all shared the common urge to repeat the exploits of the Savoy on the Priory of St John of Jerusalem, way out among the suburban fields.

The priory was the exquisite home of the Knights Hospitaller. This was a splendid building, enriched by the Hospitallers' tradition as a grand European order of crusading knights and blessed with a very pleasant position well beyond the cornfields and horse markets of Smithfield. The route passed through Holborn, where Legett had a number of houses. The rebels set fire to all of them. They also torched all of the rented properties and tenements belonging to the Hospital of St John, before they reached the priory itself. It occupied almost as large a plot as the Temple. This gave the rebels ample run to trample and destroy the buildings of the priory. They left it ablaze. Many of the outbuildings were razed and the fire that the rebels left behind was so intense that it burned for a full week.

Hostility to Hales and his order was deep-seated and intense, and he seems to have been the figure, after Gaunt, who roused the greatest and most universal hatred among all manner of rebels. Despite his short tenure at the head of the Treasury, people hated him for his dual position as the prior on the one hand of an extremely wealthy monastic order, and on the other of a royal administration that seemed financially inept to the point of corruption. Across the entire City, and right out into the countryside, property connected with him and his order attracted violence and arson.

Hales himself was safely barricaded inside the Tower with the king. No doubt he despaired at the destruction all around him, but at least the thick walls of the royal fortress protected him. Outside, a large crowd had gathered, crying out for another audience with the king. When their requests were rebuffed by the stony silence of the castle walls, they laid siege to the nearby area. The bulk of the mob gathered in the walled grounds of the Hospital of St Katherine, which was outside the City walls but directly adjacent to the south-east corner of the Tower, at the foot of the eastern half of Tower Hill. The rebels lay around in the gardens and gazed up at the great White Tower, surrounded by the crenellated walls and watchtowers that lay beyond the fort's deep moat.

The Tower had a guard of perhaps 1200 men, but its council that evening was plagued by uncertainty, insecurity and fear. There was deep division concerning the best course of action. Mayor Walworth theoretically controlled the City militia, but with so many of the rebels now drawn from the ranks of the London mob, it was by no means certain that a reliable force could be raised to clear the City of insurgents, without in the process provoking either further destruction or losing control entirely. The rebels at St Katherine's were clamouring for the surrender of their supposed enemies in the king's council, and looked to be camped out for some time. The situation was so unprecedented that the whole machinery of government had ground to a halt; all that the besieged nobles could do was to survey the destruction on all sides and despair.

As the evening wore on, Richard – uncounselled and alone – picked his way to the top of a little turret on the eastern side of the Tower and looked down into the grounds of the hospital, where his subjects lay. As he looked at them he perhaps saw, unfettered by the cynicism of his older counsellors, that their simple devotion was not mealy-mouthed; rather, it was a sincere expression of their worldview. Their adoration of him alone played directly into his burgeoning sense of self-esteem. Richard had wanted to negotiate with the rebels at Rotherhithe the previous day, and Salisbury, Sudbury and Hales' caution in forbidding this had served only to bring the danger closer to home. To prevaricate further might send another plume of smoke spiralling into the London skyline. The loss of the Tower would have rendered insignificant the terrible fates of the Savoy and the Priory of St John, both of which could be seen burning from the turrets on the opposite side of the fortress. The only option that promised any hope of resolution was to talk to the rebels.

Accordingly, Richard decided to experiment with taking charge. He sent a royal messenger down to St Katherine's to offer the rebels a deal: everyone camped there should go peaceably to their homes, and in exchange Richard was prepared to grant pardons for all the offences that they had so far committed.

To Richard it may have sounded like a plausible deal, but when the messenger stood before the rebels and announced the terms to them he was laughed away. The exhilaration of the day's destruction and the momentum of the revolt had put the rebels in a position far stronger than they had held at Rotherhithe. They would leave only, they said, in exchange for custody of the traitors in the Tower, and charters of manumission from all forms of serfdom.

Richard was in a quandary. He could not contemplate handing over his mentors and advisers, including Sudbury, the man who had crowned and anointed him, or Hales, the prior of such a prestigious and holy order as the Hospitallers. Yet he had to concede something to relieve the Tower. The next tactic he tried was one of acquiescence. He sent instructions to a royal clerk to prepare a bill.

A short while later, the rebels at St Katherine's would have been fascinated by the arrival of two royal knights, bringing with them a parchment bearing the king's personal signet seal. A space was made, and a man among them who could read was brought a chair. He stood above the crowd and read the message that had come straight from the fourteen-year-old monarch:

'Richard, king of England and France,' he began, 'gives his great thanks to his good commons, for that they have so great a desire to see and maintain their king; and he grants them pardon for all manner of trespasses and misprisions and felonies done up to this hour, and wills and commands that everyone should now quickly return to his own home.'[3]

So far, this was nothing more than had been promised by the earlier messenger, and the formulaic flattery of the king's greeting did little to sell the promise of a simple pardon as a bargaining tool. The message continued:

'He wills and commands that everyone should put his grievances in writing and have them sent to him; and he will provide, with the aid of his loyal lords and his good council, such remedy as shall be profitable both to him and to them and to the kingdom.'[4]

It was a polite fob-off. There was nothing whatsoever in the king's offer to appeal to the commons. One of their principal sources of loathing was the tendency of government towards the supremacy of the written word – so to be told that the king would not deal with them in person, but requested that they go home and submit written articles of legal complaint, was not only inadequate, it was downright insulting.

A great shout went up around the crowd that the king's bill was nothing more than a trifle and a mockery. Stirred from the evening lull, the rebels started filing back into London, crying out all around the City that all the lawyers, and anyone who could write a legal writ or a letter, were to be beheaded, wherever they could be found. Fires started beneath the houses of the first victims, and all around the City, acts of terror, murder and bloody score-settling continued. London was in uproar, and a night of chaos beckoned.

In a high garret of the Tower, the young king watched in desperation as a new set of flames rose around the City. He summoned his lords once more, to demand their counsel. The rage of the insurgent multitude had somehow to be dampened, and before the night was out, a plan of emergency action was required.

ELEVEN

WAR COUNCIL

When this party was approaching London and near a certain estate
of the Master of St John's Hospital called Highbury they saw there a
multitude of twenty thousand rustics and common people who had
set fire to the its buildings, already burning inextinguishably, and were
striving to pull down with their tools all that the fire could not destroy.
I myself saw men summoned and forced before one of the leaders of
the rebels, called 'John Strawe', who made them promise that they
would adhere to King Richard and the commons.

THOMAS WALSINGHAM

St Albans, Friday, 14 June, 4 a.m.
The bleary pre-dawn service of matins was still in progress at the
abbey of St Albans, when the monks in the abbey church heard the
noisy tramp of feet marching into town. The small monastic town
was only 25 miles north of London, and both the abbot and the
townsfolk had been well informed of the progress of the revolt.
There had been a tense, agitated air in the town for days, as news
of the rebellion had emboldened the townsfolk to take up arms
against the rule of the monastic landlords.

Now, clumping up the old Roman road through the chilly early
morning air from Barnet, there came the first deputation of rebel
messengers that the town had seen. They had marched through the
night to spread word of the glorious victories won on Corpus Christi,

to tell tales of the City in uproar, nobles scattered and confused, and the suburbs sending up tongues of jagged flame into the midsummer night sky.

The messengers from Barnet had come from territory belonging to the Essex rebels, and they spoke with an authority they claimed came straight from the rebel high command. The rebellion was spreading; the traitors in the Tower were surrounded. And now the next phase of the plan was to begin. St Albans and Barnet, demanded the messengers, must now rise, and join the bands of true commons amassed in and around the capital. They demanded that all in the town were to arm themselves with the weapons that they could best handle and set out immediately for London. The townsfolk were warned that if they were foolish enough to resist, they could expect an army of 20,000 rebels to visit, and lead them off under duress, leaving the ancient Roman settlement of St Albans nothing more than a collection of charred stumps in the ground.

Though to the monks this was a terrifying interruption to their morning's worship, to the townsfolk of St Albans the threats of arson and forced service in the rebel army were quite unnecessary. They had already caught the fever of rebellion, and gathered together quite cheerfully when Abbot Thomas de la Mare called immediately on all the residents and tenants of the abbey, whether clerical or lay, to set out for London in order to assuage the insane demands of the rebels and save their town from destruction. They had a whole litany of grievances to rehearse against the monks, and the call to arms met with an enthusiastic response.

So a strange and disparate party set out from St Albans as first light was creeping above the horizon – the monks shivering in the morning air, shaking their heads in consternation and lamenting a day of affliction, anguish, calamity and grief;[1] the townsfolk making light of their mission to swell the ranks of the insurgents. They headed south-east down Sopwell Street, past the poles where the heads of miscreants would normally be stuck, and out of the town in the direction of Barnet, and, beyond Barnet, London.

As the two parties neared the City, they came upon the manor of

Highbury, a small village to the north of the City, where Treasurer Hales was the local landlord. As the St Albans men approached, they would first have smelled woodsmoke. Then cries of a substantial crowd would have carried to them; as they came closer they would have spied a mass of figures gathered around a number of very large and beautiful houses, all ablaze, and with a multitude seemingly 20,000 strong thronging a scene of proud destruction. The stone country house was overrun by rebels; the grange and barn were burning down.

Leading the mayhem was Jack Straw. As the rebels had divided into three main parties, Straw had been given command of the contingent responsible for attacking traitors' possessions in the suburbs – it is likely that the orders to rise that were being sent to villages and towns such as St Albans were emanating from him. Straw clearly relished the task of leadership, and had taken to directing actions with the haughty zeal of a petty tyrant. He was summoning men before him to swear oaths of allegiance, and when the St Albans party were spotted arriving, they were called to Straw, and commanded to swear the familiar rebel oath: that of obedience to 'King Richard and the commons'.

Straw's style of command reflected the growing self-confidence of the rebel leadership. They had marched to London, negotiated the loyalty of the urban commons, successfully entered the City, committed with impunity all number of wanton acts of violence and destruction, laid waste the greatest palace in England, turned Cheapside into a gruesome butchering block for traitors, and gained the firm upper hand in their dealings with the royal party pinned down inside the Tower. Their strategy could not have been more effective, and with the millenarian whispers of John Ball in their ears, their ambitions began to swell.

As dawn broke around the Tower of London, there was a far more terrifying noise than the rhythmic plod of messengers' feet. The whole night had been interrupted by the yells of the rebels camped at St Katherine's. Many of them had gorged themselves on drink provided by the London commons, and on the victuals intercepted on their way for delivery to the Tower. Those who did not lie snoring in darkness clamoured, yelped and generally made as though the very devil was among them.[2] The confidence of being close to their leaders gave rise to all manner of fanciful plans. They would camp out until the king had come to them and they could embrace one another as liege lord and faithful subjects ought. Chancellor Sudbury was to be seized and commanded to make account of all the money that had been levied in taxes during the previous five years – and woe betide him should he not be able to offer a satisfactory reckoning.

Inside the Tower, the night had been understandably tense. There was a sharp divide between Richard's counsellors. The rich burgesses of London – Mayor Walworth's party – were in belligerent mood. On a personal level they would not have been entirely sorry to see John of Gaunt's possessions destroyed and his retainers hiding their badges of service in terror of the mob. But personal grievances with the duke himself were overridden by a necessary sense of class solidarity. The commons both of country and City had become a menace to property in general, and there was absolutely no guarantee that they would not turn from setting fire to properties of the Duchy of Lancaster, the Hospital of St John and the London legal profession to attacking the houses of the privileged men in the City. Mayor Walworth had already lost property in Southwark. The vast wealth and properties belonging to him and his two most prominent colleagues, Nicholas Brembre and the greatest magnate merchant of them all, John Philipot, were obvious targets for the jealous London rebels; and the Guildhall might be next to feel the lick of flames if their grudge against certain lords mutated into a grudge against all forms of lordship.

With these concerns for their property and the good governance of the City in mind, Walworth's party had pressed hard on the king during the night's debates for a clean, sharp strike against the rebels. He, Brembre and Philipot had all been active in the military defence of the City – in 1378 Philipot had, in fact, kitted out at his own expense a sea defence party that had vanquished Scottish pirate ships with remarkable success. They were no soft-handed money-men, but hard-bitten merchant oligarchs who were more than capable of military ruthlessness in the name of protecting their financial interests. And here their interests were threatened as never before. Walworth had argued that with many of the rebels dead drunk, a raiding party split into four might issue out of the Tower, take the City by four different entrances and slay the rebels while they slept. They were poorly armed and full of wine, said Walworth, bluntly – and in such a sorry state they might be killed like flies.

Furthermore, argued Walworth, the veteran soldier Sir Robert Knolles was bristling in his home, guarding his treasure and ready to leap into action with 120 well-armed men at his disposal. Knolles was a war captain of immense experience and repute, whose yeoman stock and vast wealth, earned through a glittering thirty-five-year career on the front line of the Hundred Years War, had earned him close ties to the City. He owned property all around London, and would have been able to monitor closely the movements of rebels both inside and outside the walls from his manor of St Pancras and houses in Islington, Kentish Town to the north, Barking and All Hallows to the east and St Giles Cripplegate, which lay within earshot of the butchering block at Cheapside. He had fought in some of the bloodiest encounters of the century and survived – with his leadership and the assistance of the famous French knight Sir Perducas d'Albret, who could also command a loyal force if necessary. The increasingly deranged rebels might be vanquished in one swift, bloody cull.

With evening bringing a temporary lull, Walworth's plan had appealed as a decisive move of the sort sorely lacking since the first word of revolt had come back from Brentwood in late May. But to the majority of Richard's counsellors, an overnight raid through the City represented a gamble whose consequences did not justify the risk. It was becoming clear that this was no invading force, and that the fomenting elements were drawn as much from the City itself as from the rural invaders. As had been made abundantly clear since the early days of the rebellion – when the social compact was broken and the common multitude forgot the duty of service and respect for lordly hierarchy – their numbers told. So cautious heads around the king had outweighed the proactive scheming of Walworth, Brembre and Philipot, arguing that until the London commons could be relied upon to remain loyal, there could be no strike against the insurgents.

Salisbury – a soldier of similar age to Knolles, and another of Edward III's old captains – was one of the foremost of these cautious voices. He had been characteristically shrewd in all his advice to Richard, since accompanying him on the expedition to Blackheath on Wednesday afternoon; now he advocated a policy of reason towards the rebels. He had recent experience of siege tactics, and eight years previously had managed to relieve the famous siege of Brest, purely through negotiation. Though he was certainly not unduly circumspect by nature, and had, in his thirty-five years of military service, put to the sword far better-organised forces than the current rabble. He had counselled the young king that in the present circumstances it was better to grant the rebels everything they asked, appease them with a show of fairness, and take the sting out of the movement. The alternative was to be dragged into a fight that, with such a small party of men, they might not win – the loss of which might end in catastrophe, ruin and disinheritance.

In the end, Salisbury's caution had won the night. Unlike his father, who had led an army into battle at Crécy when he was a teenager, Richard was not a precocious commander, and he lacked the experience and mettle to throw caution to the wind and attack. Walworth, outranked by the superior nobility of the more timid party, was commanded to sit on his hands. Nevertheless, as the Tower had settled down for the night, the City divided into commotion and slumber alike, it had been resolved that dawn should open on the last day of the rebellion.

The Gough Map of Britain, c.1360
By the fourteenth century, ordinary Englishmen had a sense of
their realm as a whole, and would rise to defend its interest.

LEFT: *Shearing sheep*
The wool trade was an important part of the English economy, particularly in the south-east heartlands of the revolt.

ABOVE: *Travelling by harvest cart*
Part of the rebels' success was their ability to move quickly around the countryside – which must have been accomplished on horseback or by cart.

LEFT: *Sowing seeds later to be reaped*
The rhythms and festivals of agriculture still governed rural life in England.

ABOVE: *Ploughing with oxen*
For all that the world after the Black Death promised, working the land could still be a life of unremitting toil.

RIGHT: *A cook at work*
Meal times were an important opportunity for the lower orders to exchange information and ideas.

BELOW: *Stacking corn*
Rural life required interdependence, and community ties were very strong in medieval England. The revolt spread through existing village structures.

LEFT: *Geoffrey Chaucer*
He lived above the
Aldgate in London and
described the hellish
noise of Tyler's rebels
massacring the
Flemings.

BELOW: *William
Blake's nineteenth-
century impression of
the pilgrim road to
Canterbury*
Tyler's army marched
the road en route to
Blackheath.

John of Gaunt, Duke of Lancaster He was despised by City dignitaries and rank-and-file rebels alike.

A romanticised image of William Walworth, Mayor of London
He was vastly wealthy, a fishmonger and an oligarch.

ABOVE: *Lesnes Abbey*
The remains of one of the Essex
and Kent rebels' first targets.
(It was dissolved and destroyed
under Henry VIII.)

RIGHT: *King Richard II (1377–1399),*
last of the Plantagenets.
His reign was beset by rebellion,
political intrigue, failed war
and constitutional crisis.

John Ball leads the rebels against the government
An idealised image from the Chronicles of Jean Froissart, who described the revolt in detail.

The King meets his subjects
Richard II attempts to negotiate with Tyler's men at Rotherhithe
on Wednesday 12th June, 1381.

ABOVE: *The Savoy Palace*
A seventeenth-century image of the Savoy Palace as it would have appeared to Londoners in 1380.

LEFT: *The destruction of the Savoy Palace*
Another late image, this time showing Queen Joan, Richard II's mother, pleading with the rebels as the Savoy burned.

Sudbury and Hales are killed
There are similarities with popular images of the martyrdom
of St Thomas à Becket, another murdered archbishop.

LEFT: *Wat Tyler attacks a poll tax collector*
A late, romanticised and fictional image, but a profound representation of rebellion.

BELOW: *The showdown at Smithfield*
Tyler is run through, before the teenage king captivates and disperses his rebellious subjects.

A nineteenth-century version of Tyler's death
To many later artists, this was the defining image of a tragic episode in English history.

King Henry IV (1399–1413)
John of Gaunt's son, and Richard II's cousin. He was saved from
certain death in the Tower by a vigilant guardsman.

JACK CADE *in* Cannon Street *declaring himself* LORD *of the* CITY *of* LONDON.

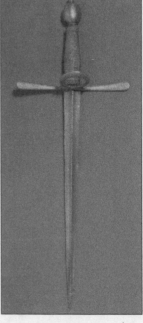

John Gower
The gloomy poet of the rebellion. He witnessed the riots and
wrote a long account of their vicious course.

TWELVE

MILE END

At that time the crowd of rustics was divided into three separate sections, one of which (as we have seen) was busy destroying the manor of Highbury. A second band waited in London in the place called 'le Mile End', while a third occupied Tower Hill ... And the king, being in a quandary, allowed the rebels to enter the Tower and to search the most secret places there at their wicked will ...

THOMAS WALSINGHAM

Mile End Road, Friday, 14 June, 7 a.m.

For the first time in the week, Aldgate Street bore human traffic passing eastwards out of the City, rather than westwards towards it. There was a tramp of feet and a clattering of hoofs as large bands of men from the countryside piled back out through the old gate and on to London's summer sports fields.

They had been sent there by Richard himself. After having spent the night in fraught deliberations with his council in the Tower, while the rebels made a din outside, Richard had summoned up the courage to take some sort of positive action. In a policy that combined the spirit of Salisbury's softly-softly approach to negotiation with Walworth's desire to meet the rebels head-on, Richard had commanded the mayor to have the sheriff and aldermen of London announce to their wards that everyone between the ages of fifteen and sixty should leave the City and make their way out to Mile End to meet him at seven of the bell.

It was a fairly straightforward idea. For the royal party, Mile End was a convenient trot north-east from the Tower, comfortingly close to the City, yet far enough away to count as neutral territory. Richard would have hoped that, for the rebels, it would seem a point of familiarity and safety; it was where the Essex camp had made their base during the second week of the revolt, and so they would feel they were finally receiving the king according to their own terms. And if the rebels could all be lured away from the Tower by following Richard himself as bait, then the siege would be lifted and some of the council might be able to escape. All they had to reckon on was the rebels wanting to meet their king more than they wanted to kill his servants.

So Richard took a large party of knights and nobles from the Tower, leaving behind only those who were thought to be most at risk of assassination. In this moment of crisis, it would have seemed like a rather meagre crowd. His two half-brothers, Thomas and John Holland, rode alongside the king, accompanied by the earls of Warwick and Oxford, and Oxford's kinsman Sir Aubrey de Vere, who carried the royal sword. The soldiers Sir Robert Knolles and Sir Thomas Percy, and the mayor, were also in tow. Behind the party, riding in a whirligig rather than on horseback, came Princess Joan, mother of Richard and of the Holland boys.

If Richard had hoped to play the saviour, leading his entire people out to the promised land, it was clear as soon as they set out from the Tower that his people were less willing to play along. The royal party was forced to cut a path through the streets with the rebel crowd swarming all around, rowdy and intimidating. In a sheriff's report compiled eighteen months after the revolt, it was recorded that the London captain Thomas Farringdon managed to push his way close enough to Richard to make a grab for the reins of his horse. In a show of exceptional rudeness, Farringdon raged at the king, shouting out demands for revenge on 'that false traitor the prior' – a reference to Hales. Already the policy of leaving the treasurer in the Tower seemed to be a wise one. Notwithstanding the general hatred of Hales on the basis of his political position, Farringdon was additionally believed to hold a personal grudge against him, born of some obscure dispute over property. As Richard trotted onwards towards the City limits, Farringdon told the king that if he could not obtain royal recompense then he was now 'strong enough to take justice on my own account'.[1]

It was not just Richard who was harassed. Walworth's ally Nicholas Brembre was spotted in the royal train by a brewer called William Trewman, who began shouting threats at him. Probably he was warning Brembre that he could expect to find his luxurious life and wealth in the City under threat, because later that day the same Trewman would visit Brembre's houses and extort money from the inhabitants with extreme menace.

This kind of behaviour should have been acutely worrying. There was a sense that the rebellion was starting to fray around the edges as the main focus on protesting the realm's misgovernment was joined by numerous examples of petty rivalry and jealousy. The crowd was so intimidating that the queen mother's nerve failed and her whirligig turned back for the safety of the Tower. But despite the fracas, Richard seems to have maintained his princely calm.

When they arrived at Mile End, Richard and his followers saw once again a great sea of subjects, clamouring for his arrival. The mob from London was being joined by roaming gangs from all over the counties – and piebald conventicles from Essex, Hertfordshire and Suffolk had all travelled down to join the fun.

At each encounter with the rebels, Richard would have seen a more dirty and disorderly rabble. They were still arranged under the pennons and banners of a loyal army, but in his eyes the comparison even between here and two days earlier, at Rotherhithe, would not have been favourable. Two days of sleeping rough, indulging in London's bacchanalian pleasures and cavorting among burning buildings would have left them filthy and hung over. Various trophies were borne aloft on sticks and pikes: Richard may have seen with surprise two books bobbing above the crowd. They belonged to Edmund de la Mare, the admiral of the east coast. They had been stolen by one group of Essex rebels who had taken the tour to London via the villages of Essex's eastern seaboard and they were impaled on the double prongs of a pitchfork. The rebels here were at first noisy and disjointed. There were attacks on the property surrounding Mile End all morning and scuffles and fights were breaking out across the fields between rival companies – at least one Kent man was killed there that day.[2] Richard must have looked at his subjects – this adoring, muddy rabble – and felt his lordly benevolence erring rather close to simple disgust.

He should also have started to feel extremely uneasy. For there were some important absentees from the rebel ranks. As with the royal party, the rebel party was incomplete. There was no Tyler, no Ball, and no Straw.[3] In fact, if Richard could have stepped out and enquired among the Mile End crowd at large, he would have found that this was by no means a representative mob. The most radical rebels were not there. Rather, they had remained in London, lingering around the Tower and keeping a keen eye out for any sign of movement within.

For the commons who had travelled to Mile End, however, this was the moment they had been waiting for. The foremost leaders of those who had made it to Mile End came before Richard, their knees bent in supplication to their king, flags of their loyalty fluttering above the crowd behind them. To them, this must undoubtedly have registered as the greatest moment of their lives. The king could be expected to remain, in the lives of all but the grandest of subjects, an enigmatic totem. So to approach him and to approach with permission to discuss freely with him their place in the world and the course of his reign, was an unimaginable honour.

Richard asked them what they wanted, what they lacked, and why they had come to London. The reply he received was straightforward and heartfelt. It was a request for a countryside charter of justice. They asked him to make them free for ever – themselves, their lands and their heirs. They asked that all the men in the realm of England be made of free condition, and that all those of future generations should live free from the yoke of servitude. They asked, specifically, for a rent limit of 4d per acre, which meant in effect a limit to the financial power of the landlords and an end to the oppressions of cash payments through rents, feudal and semi-feudal fines, through the manor courts, through the royal courts, and most recently through the tax system of royal government. Finally, they asked that no man should be compelled to work except by employment under a regularly reviewed contract.[4]

In the light of the violence and rising hysteria that had gripped London under the reign of the rural peasants and the rebellious City commons, this was a remarkably lucid and reasonable set of demands. There were no calls for the heads of nobles, nor for any purge of government – all that was requested of the king, in simple but intelligent terms, was a reassurance that the creeping tendency towards a legal form of serfdom should be halted, and that a legal framework protecting the rights to free labour be set up. They took issue not so much with serfdom, but with the threat of serfdom, and the whole principle of the commons of England being bullied by the royal law that ought in fact to have been protecting them. The Mile End peasants gave their king a succinct account of their grievances, and asked for reasonable, limited demands founded on their simple concept of natural justice, but pragmatic enough for consideration in the world they saw around them.

If he was surprised by what the rebels had asked – whether its boldness or its lucidity – Richard did not show it. He was at Mile End not as a true negotiator, but as a lure. Whatever the rebels had demanded Richard would that morning most likely have granted. He and his party had come to Mile End with the whole purpose of buying off a large portion of the crowd by a policy of appeasement. Though it was disconcerting that not all the rebels had vacated the City, it must still have come as a relief that he was not being pressed to agree to anything more radical, unrealistic or deranged.

To reward the commons before him, the king had the rebels arrayed in two long ranks. As they shuffled into order, Richard had it proclaimed to all that he would guarantee their freedom as they requested, and that it should be confirmed by charters secured by the royal seal. If they wanted freedom, all they needed to do was to wait in line and take their new charter of liberties.

If he had ended his Mile End speech with that, Richard would have played his hand perfectly. The revolt, which had threatened utter calamity, would be about to go out with a whimper.

But Richard did not end there. Either drunk on the calming effect his words seemed to have on the rebels, or else feeling an inexperienced negotiator's urge to push compromise too hard, he told the commons that in addition to the charters, they were all free to go across the realm of England catching traitors, whom they should bring before him to be tried according to due process of law.

In saying this, he undid all the good work that had preceded. It was a damning indictment of the quality of his counsel that he was allowed to offer of his own volition this extraordinary and provocative promise. It was a massive blunder, and by granting the rebels the radical demands he had expected them to make, rather than the relatively conservative demands that he in fact received, he changed the whole character of the revolt. Word quickly spread among the crowd that the king had sanctioned the taking of rebel enemies. Almost instantly, companies began detaching, leaving Mile End to join the vanguard staking out Tower Hill. It was no secret where the 'traitors' were holed up, and with royal sanction for their arrest, there was only the Tower drawbridge to save them.

Richard, as he watched the companies detach, dissolving back into their apparent disorder and hollering around word of what had just happened, would have hoped with all his heart that Sudbury and Hales – as well as everyone else who was stuck in the Tower, a group that included his mother and his young cousin Henry of Derby – had managed to board the boats on the Thames. But in truth he had no idea. He had given the rebels a blank charter to storm the Tower; now it was only to be hoped they would find it empty. The royal party set off back for the City, towards their new base of Baynard's Castle, and all must have prayed that they would not soon be watching the destruction of their former fortress.

THIRTEEN

THE TOWER

A little later the executioners entered crying, 'Where is that traitor to the kingdom? Where is the despoiler of the people?' The archbishop was not at all disturbed and replied to their shouts: 'Good my sons, you have come; behold, I am the archbishop whom you seek, but not a traitor or a despoiler.' On seeing him, those limbs of Satan laid their impious hands on him and tore him from the Chapel . . .

THOMAS WALSINGHAM

The Tower of London, Friday, 14 June, 9 a.m.

In the Chapel of St John the Evangelist, the dense scent of incense hung in the air, and the thick stonework was lit irregularly by the flicker of candlelight. Backed by the solemn song of a chorister, Archbishop Sudbury's voice echoed around the chamber, filling it with the quick, calm patter of Latin devotion.[1]

This was Sudbury's second Mass of the day; he had sung his first before the king at sunrise, and later confessed Treasurer Hales and others of the royal party. He would have been tired from a sleepless night of prayer. And he was not alone. Richard and his entourage had left the Tower in a state of profound gloom, as they headed out into the unknown to their showdown with the rebels at Mile End; those left behind faced the dangerous uncertainty of escaping a siege that seemed harder to hold with each hour that passed.

Ever since Wednesday evening, when he had sat, shocked, on the

117

barge to Rotherhithe, looking out upon the throng that bayed for the young king's approval in executing their archbishop, Sudbury had known that of all the royal party, it was he who faced the greatest danger. Vandalism and destruction had been wreaked on his property and palaces, from Canterbury to Southwark. His name came second only to John of Gaunt's on the list of traitors to be executed by the rebels – and the experience of having seen it written down when messages were being exchanged with the Kent rebels at Blackheath must have been sickening. It was well known that he and Hales were blamed personally by the rebels for squandering the tax that had been raised to pursue the war with France. This, combined with some latent anticlerical feeling in the crowds that thronged through the streets and suburbs of London, and the total disregard in which they seemed to hold the sanctity of churches when hunting down their victims, must have expelled from Sudbury's intelligent mind any hope of mercy if he were to be caught.

Now, despite the cool of the chapel, that prospect was loud and very close at hand. The sweaty, dirty, dangerous cabal of vagabonds strutted about like peacocks on the green swell of Tower Hill, an arrow's flight away from the place where he now stood and prayed among the wisps of waxy candle smoke. And the ringleader of these tormentors was a man with whom Sudbury was intimately acquainted: John Ball.

Sudbury would not have missed the irony of being imprisoned at Ball's hands. Ball had dogged Sudbury's footsteps over his distinguished career, cropping up like a virulent weed in churches, churchyards, markets and highways, travelling the country preaching his dangerous and unorthodox dogma of equality, told through the quasi-mystical language of the peasant oral tradition, which was rich with cryptic allegory and the rhythms of traditional song, and drawing his audience into his web of apostasy. No matter how hard Sudbury had tried to squash him, he had reappeared, not with the intellectual tenacity or the theological sophistication of the troublesome Oxford don John Wyclif, but with a command of popular thought and the powerful ability to aggravate social tension through bogus religious rhetoric and relentless sermonising.

In April, Sudbury had managed to imprison Ball for the third time in fifteen years, excommunicating him for the fourth time and writing to the secular authorities in outrage at Ball's schismatic and erroneous pronouncements, his heretical depravity, and his poisonous influence as a malevolent shepherd misleading the English flock.[2]

But now Ball was loose and Sudbury was the quarry. Inside the Tower chapel, the archbishop solemnly finished the Mass and took Holy Communion.

Elsewhere in the Tower, the mood was just as sombre. Those left out of the Mile End party included Treasurer Hales, a number of courtiers most closely associated with Gaunt – including his son Derby – and several politically sensitive royal counsellors, including the widely loathed John Legge, who was charged by the rebels with being the author of the policy of farming out poll tax investigative commissions for the profit of royal favourites.

The composition of the group left in the Tower was informed by two considerations – first, that it would be dangerous and inflammatory for the king to take these provocative targets with him to Mile End, where the sight of their arch-enemies might incite the rebels to clash with the royal party; and second, that the best chance for Sudbury, Hales and the rest to escape was for them to hope they could use Richard's absence from the Tower as cover for their getaway.

But as the morning had passed, and the uneasy still that Richard had left behind settled over the Tower, it became clear that escape was not an option. Queen Joan had returned from the trip to Mile End and would have reported the sorry news that the rebels were not to be herded as though they were sheep. She would have seen that while a large, ribald party had followed the king out of the Aldgate to Mile End, the most radical elements had remained by the Tower, eyeing the prizes that they knew lay inside. Tyler, Ball and Straw were, presumably, at that moment outside the Tower, heading a band composed of men from villages that had been active in the rebellion since its inception. Lookouts kept close watch on all exits from the Tower – and when movement just after dawn had been spotted on the escape jetty, an old woman with her eyes trained on the river raised such a racket that all hope of immediate escape was lost.

Without a recognised military leader among the Tower party (Salisbury, Knolles and Walworth, the three surest heads, were with the king), morale had plummeted among the 180 or so archers and guards who were left quite literally to hold the fort in the king's absence. For the last day or so, taunting parties of rebels had camped out on Tower Hill, pointing out their mastery of the capital, and the futility of continuing to hold out against those who had achieved so much so quickly that weekend, and implying that the guards were traitors for protecting enemies of the country. Supplies had dried up, as the rebels enforced an aggressive blockade against the king's victuals – as much to feed themselves on royal supplies as to inconvenience the defenders of the Tower. The rebels were used to breaking castles and prisons by psychological warfare, rather than with battering rams, and now it seemed that London's great fortress, which days before had seemed the safest place in the city, was suddenly an island.

As the morning wore on, the threats from across the Tower ditch, a moat that siphoned from the Thames a broad, cold, murky wall of water, became louder and more urgent. Ball's railing and vitriol had long since taken seed among the assembled rebels, and they could smell blood. Pressing close to the Tower drawbridge, they began to harangue the guards on the gate. Behind the mob on the moat, plumes of smoke and the occasional collapse of burning buildings in the continuing melee would have given the impression that all of London was close to lost – a rumour that was, by this stage, becoming ever more believable. The Tower's last guards looked out on the wonder and despaired.

Their desperation undid the Tower. It could have been physically held against the rebels, but the guards' minds were fragile, and a fatal paralysis of the spirit overcame them. When word came back from Mile End that Richard had acquiesced before the demands of the Essex rebels and given his permission for the punishment of traitors, it not only emboldened the besiegers, but broke the hearts of the besieged. The worst fears of those left in the Tower were realised: the king had forsaken them in the name of saving the City. Seemingly without even a show of resistance, the drawbridge came down.

The rebels flocked in. As they passed by the pathetic guards, the archers and war veterans who should have been holding the royal fortress until the bitter end, they tousled their hair and pulled playfully on their beards.[3] Gnarled hands holding filthy sticks prodded at the hapless defenders and the gleeful rebels began to run into the bedrooms and cupboards of the Tower. They ran into rooms and bounced on the beds, joking and laughing among themselves as they did so. There was banter with the dejected soldiers, who were invited – with a cheeky smile – to be friends.

At least one party began to force locks on doors that looked as if they might conceal legal repositories; but the main object here was not more records for the bonfire, but living, breathing victims.[4]

Sheer terror broke out among the inhabitants, as they scrambled for safety. Henry of Derby survived only because a soldier helped conceal him from the invaders. (Derby never forgot this kindness, and years later, when he himself was king, rewarded the soldier that had saved him.) The queen mother, in the company of other ladies of the court, swooned when the ruffians broke in, and was smuggled out to a waiting barge. But others were not so lucky. Hales was found, as was Legge. Derby was fortunate to be hidden, because anyone connected to Gaunt was also captured. But as chaos reigned in the hallways of the Tower, the duty soldiers stood helpless, and the rebels rounded up their traitors with impunity.

In the chapel, Sudbury would have heard the commotion and sensed that his time had come. Yet the devotions continued. As voices echoed around the Tower's corridors, Sudbury chanted the *Commendatio*, the *Placebo* and the *Dirige* – common medieval prayers for the dead. As the clattering and the thuds of knobbled staves on the thick, bolted doors of the Tower grew louder and closer, he chanted the Seven Psalms – penitential passages that called on God for forgiveness, remission of sins and protection from enemies. And as the rough laughter of the invaders mingled with the screams of those inside the Tower who had been uncovered from their hiding spots and marched out to face the wrath of the crowds assembled on Tower Hill, Sudbury sucked down still more lungfuls of the scented chapel air and began to chant the litany – the long, imploring catalogue of requests for protection, forgiveness and prayer from all the holy saints of the Church.

As he reached the end of this long stream of requests to individual saints, the chapel door flew open, and the commons burst in, accompanied by a minor official who had been intimidated into leading them to the archbishop.

'*Omnes sancti orate pro nobis,*' were the last words that Sudbury could muster[5] – 'all the holy saints, pray for us' – as the gang crossed the chapel floor and hustled him through the corridors of the Tower, some with their hands on his hood and his arms, others delivering what threats and blows to his anointed person they could. He was bundled past the raucous crowds that had bullied their way into the inner sanctum of the royal fortress, and out into the daylight.

It was said afterwards that Sudbury argued with his captors – imploring them to accept that he was no traitor, and no plunderer, but their archbishop. What sin had he committed? he asked. What good could come of destroying their prelate? He told them that such a deed would bring down nothing but the wrath of God and the Pope, and would lead to an interdict over the whole of England.[6]

But his arguments flew up and over the rebels like dust in the morning breeze. Sudbury would have realised that his fate was sealed. His hooded head bowed, he was shoved at the head of a train of helpless victims to the top of Tower Hill. He saw Hales, Legge, and one of Gaunt's servants lined up and ready to face the same doom.

It is just possible that Sudbury remembered Psalm 42, a popular beginning to the mass, and one that no doubt he had had cause to recite regularly, and perhaps even on that very day:

Judica me, Deus, et
discerne causam meam
de gente non sancta: ab

homine iniquo et doloso
erue me.

[...]

Emitte lucem tuam et
veritatem tuam: ipsa me
deduxerunt et
adduxerunt in montem
sanctum tuum, et in
tabernacula tua.

Et introibo ad altare
Dei: ad Deum qui
laetificat juventutem
meam . . .

Its elegant Latin would have sounded splendid in the dark hush of a royal chapel – the vernacular, though, is just as poignant:

Do me justice, O God, and
fight my fight
against an unholy people,
rescue me from the wicked
and deceitful man.

[...]

Send forth Thy light
and thy truth: for they
have led me and
brought me to thy holy
hill and Thy dwelling
place.

And I will go to the
altar of God, to God, the
joy of my youth.

Sudbury knelt amid the rabble on Tower Hill, and as the first blow of the axe fell, blood-curdling screams went up from the crowd. Then there was nothing but the crunch of iron through flesh and bone; the savage butchering of the archbishop; the ashen resignation of the rest of the shocked captives, and the beginnings of descent into chaos and inferno.

FOURTEEN

THE RUSTICS RAMPANT

> They yelledon, as feendes doon in helle
> The dokes cryden, as men wolde hem quelle,
> The gees, for feere, flowen over the trees;
> Out of the hyve cam the swarm of bees;
> So hydous was the noyse, ah *benidicite*!
> Certes, he Jakke Strawe and his meynee
> Ne made never shoutes halfe so shrille
> When that they wolden any Flemyng kille . . .
>
> GEOFFREY CHAUCER

Charing, near London, Friday, 14 June, 11 a.m.
The road out of London to the royal village of Westminster was
scarred and burned, littered with the smoking remains of Thursday's
mayhem. Any wisp of a summer breeze would have stirred across the
road the ash and debris that was all that remained of the palace of
the Savoy. Boundary walls and hedgerows had been left jagged and
ruined from the assaults of the rampant mob, while rooftops were
rent through with holes made by the hands of Wat Tyler's irreverent
apprentices.

London's dignitaries quaked inside those houses and inns that had
escaped rebel punishment. Word of Richard's decision to grant the
rebels the freedom to hunt traitors had begun to filter throughout
the city and its suburbs, and the paralysis that had characterised

London's initial reaction to the rebel invasion would by now have turned to outright terror.

Though the day was young, the morning's events had profoundly transformed the nature and character of the rebellion. The rustics were rampant. Any former sheen of honesty, zeal and righteous discipline was no more. Their band had split – divided and radicalised – in the aftermath of Mile End, and those who remained in London were emboldened and openly bloodthirsty.[1]

The repercussions of Richard's naive charter of endorsement, which was now being copied out by a team of thirty royal scribes and circulated about the City, were twofold. In the first place, the desired effect of drawing to a close the rebels' mission had been a partial success. Flocks of rebels from the Essex and Hertfordshire villages had taken the Mile End meeting to be the end point of their excursion and set off back for their homes, elated at the success of their mission, admiring the simple justice of their child king. Some waited to receive their royal charters, others just made for home. In total perhaps one half of the rebels bade farewell to the City in which they had revelled, and departed for the security of familiar comforts: the village, the summer rhythm of feast days and games, the farm and the Church. The main road up to Colchester would have teemed with hungry, ragged, happy faces; the air would have thickened with exchanged stories of an incredible adventure.

But on the other side of London, on the ruined road to Westminster, the radicals stalked. Anyone brave enough to have stood by the Eleanor Cross in the hamlet of Charing would have seen an awful procession bumping along the highway. A crowd of rebels marched beneath a gruesome banner. Five lances pierced the morning sky, and on each was the butchered head of a servant of the Crown.[2]

First among the grisly relics was the head of Archbishop Sudbury. It had taken eight blows from an inexpert executioner to decapitate him, leaving his neck an ugly mess, the spinal column more likely crushed and torn than cut clean through. There would have been blood spattered across his face from the second blow he suffered; the first had been so unskilled that it had merely opened a gash in his neck. Onlookers had heard him cry out that this was the hand of God, and when the second blow had fallen, he had instinctively raised his own fingers to touch the wound. The executioner, excited but hopelessly inaccurate, had chopped off the ends of his ringed fingers. Now the bloodied head sat on top of a pole; above, the *coup de grâce* – Sudbury's red mitre nailed on to his skull.

Around him were the four heads of the others killed alongside him: Hales; Legge; John of Gaunt's physician, William Appleton; and a juror, identified by City records after the revolt as Richard Somenour of Stebenhithe (Stepney).[3] They bobbed along like grotesque puppets.

Were these the heads of traitors? Or were the traitors those who waved the poles about, banded together in a sinister procession down towards the royal village? Richard's approval of the rebel manhunt had now muddied the waters to the point where legally – and indeed morally – both sides of the argument stood open. Prior to Mile End, the rebels had, by and large, held back from indiscriminate slaughter, and upheld a strict code with regard to the property they targeted, and their behaviour when they were attacking it, for it would have been clear to them that they must behave in accordance with the just principles that underpinned the revolt. Now, though, the king had brought all of their previous actions within the compass of natural, equitable law, and handed to them in written form a charter that legitimised their pursuit of 'traitors' and effectively gave them the power to decide whom exactly that included. The charter's polite request that these 'traitors' be brought before the king to be tried was an unenforceable trifle.

In short, Richard may as well have handed a blank charter to the rebels, upon which they could write his approval for any act they chose. Murders became executions. Assaults became punishments. Treachery became justice. And the pilgrimage of bloodied heads down to the king's favourite holy spot at Westminster[4] was both a repulsive subversion of the Corpus Christi parades of the previous day and a nightmarish parody of the hated judicial circuits.

Richard would have seen the gruesome parade pass close to the walls of the Royal Wardrobe, where he had ridden at great haste following the Mile End conference, having left the Tower, with its unfortunate inmates, to fall.[5] The Wardrobe was in the ward of Castle Baynard, in the south-west corner of the walled City, an area normally under the control of Alderman John Redyng. The rebels' route through the City and towards the Ludgate very probably passed along Carter Lane, the passageway between the Wardrobe and St Paul's Cathedral – if so, then the noise and the horror could not have escaped any of the royal party.[6]

With the spectacular failure – both in concept and in execution – of their strategy to defuse the revolt, Richard and his court were now so paralysed by fear that it was all they could do just to watch the bloody heads of two most senior royal ministers bob past on lances. Some would have begun to rue the fact that they had not countenanced the belligerent solutions suggested by Mayor Walworth.

Their hand was now even weaker than before. There was nothing to be done to halt the progress of the procession of heads; and the other half of the rebels also had to be served with hundreds of charters freeing them to do as they pleased across the realm. The king was forced to pass the Great Seal, so recently relinquished by his late Chancellor Archbishop, into the hands of Richard Fitzalan, earl of Arundel, who was handed the unenviable first task of overseeing the production line of charters being hastily copied out by the royal scribes, and distributed from the royal party's new base.

Outside in the City, with the people emboldened by the timorousness of the royal government, any fragile order that had persisted now dissolved into anarchy. While Sudbury's head was taken on its pilgrimage to Westminster, gangs of rebels (composed both of radical rural rebels and the ebullient London commons) began to roam the streets in broad daylight, seeking out all the 'traitors' they could.

By the time the heads returned from their journey to Westminster Abbey, at least four more murders had taken place, all by beheading. The heads were carried triumphantly in procession to London Bridge, the usual spot above which dismembered bodies were impaled as a warning to would-be peacebreakers. Sudbury's head, with its red mitre still nailed in place, was set the highest and most central. Around it went Hales, Legge, Somenour, Appleton and the four new trophies.

The heads above the bridge gate symbolised the humiliation of the City and the royal government. With the physical manifestation of rebel law in place, chaos reigned. Mobs charged through the streets. Personal vendettas started to be played out. Disputes that had rumbled along for years were suddenly settled, violently. One rebel, Thomas Raven of Rochester, made his way from Tower Hill, where he had been in the crowd when Hales was beheaded, and went to the house of Reginald Allen, a grocer to whom he was heavily indebted, and forced him to give up the bond that proved the debt.[7] Another group of rebels, containing relatively wealthy and prominent men from a number of Essex villages, including Manningtree, in the very north of the county, set about the property and houses of John Butterwick, the undersheriff of Middlesex, who lost property that afternoon in Knightsbridge, Ebury and Westminster – all well beyond the City walls.[8]

Unscrupulous members of the better ranks of London society seized the day of chaos to pursue their own feuds. Sir Robert Allen, a fishmonger, co-opted a band of Kent rebels to help him evict another of his trade, Hugh Ware, from a house he claimed to own.[9] A brewer, Walter ate Keye, spent much of the afternoon desperately hunting for a mysterious document known as the 'Jubilee Book', leading a mob who contemplated burning down the Guildhall in their hunt to destroy it.[10] All over the City, hundreds of cases frustrated in the law courts or driven by private hatred and political vendetta were pursued according to the rules of the angry mob, and resolved in the climate of terror and lawlessness.

Under mob rule, there were groups in the City who would feel especially vulnerable to attack. Chief among them were foreigners. Medieval London was home to significant populations of Genoans, Lombards and other Italian merchants, and traders from the Hanse (German and Baltic states). Foreigners often traded under royal protection or favour, frequently to the perceived detriment and chagrin of the native merchants, who felt themselves undercut by the economic favours afforded the foreigners by governments that, from the 1370s, sold export duty exemptions to foreigners as a (short-sighted) source of quick income.

One of the most prominent of these alien communities was the Flemings. As a group, they were responsible for the bulk of the cross-Channel trade that was carried out between England and the Continent.[11] Beside the merchant tensions, there was a strain of xenophobia against them, including the popular belief that they were responsible for running London's brothels.[12] And they must have been aware that they were at serious risk when order – particularly royal order – was lost.

The Flemings and their families, mirroring the guilds of London which tended to ghettoise themselves in different areas of the City according to their trades, had found their home in the Vintry, along the north bank of the Thames, clustered around the two churches of St Martin-in-the-Vintry and St James Garlickhithe, about one third of a mile upstream from London Bridge, where the heads of the murdered ministers were now displayed. Around the churches and down to the wharves on the bank of the river, there were large cellared houses, originally built by the great Bordeaux Gascon wine merchants in the earlier part of the century.[13]

It was in this area that a large gang descended. They crowded around the church of St Martin-in-the-Vintry, where word had spread that a number of Flemings were taking shelter from the anarchy. When the first rebels burst through the church doors, they found forty or more foreigners huddling inside, terrified for their lives. Showing no respect for the sanctity of their refuge – that Rubicon had been crossed too long ago – the mob seized any Fleming they could, and dragged them into the street, where the beheadings began.

In La Royal, or the Queen's Wardrobe, the royal residence in London just a few hundred yards up the road, the queen mother would have been able to hear the horrible screams of the mob, and their butchered victims, as the massacre began. What she wondered about the wisdom of her young son and his advisers, huddled in Castle Baynard, overseeing a production line of pardons and charters, as the bodies began to pile up, and the streets ran with blood, we can only guess.

One of the voices that rang through the melee was one she might have recognised: that of Richard Lyons, the fantastically rich London merchant. Lyons had been notorious in London since he had found disgrace in 1376 for colluding to the point of corruption with the court of Queen Joan's father-in-law, Edward III. Though shamed in Parliament, Lyons was an intimate of the court she would have known while her late husband, Edward the Black Prince, was alive. Though Edward had not approved of the morally wavering merchant, Queen Joan would undoubtedly have been familiar with him as a fixture of London society. Lyons lived in the opulent trading heart of Vintry, and it was from here that the mob snatched him.

Lyons knew he was a target for rebels inside London and farther afield. He had probably heard that on Wednesday his manor at Liston, near Melford, in Suffolk, had been attacked by a rebel band under John Wrawe, the captain of the most dangerous band in that county, who was that day hunting down the rebellion's third great target: John Cavendish, the Chief Justice of the Court of King's Bench, and the most senior judge in England.

With his property at risk, so was Lyons' person. When the London gangs arrived in the Vintry, they tore him from his house and pulled him through the rich streets of Cordwainer ward, to Cheapside. From his effigy in St James Garlickhithe we know the rebels were hunting for a man

> very fair and large, with his hair rounded by his ears and curled, a little beard forked; a gown, girt to him down to his feet, of branched damask, wrought with the likeness of flowers; a large purse on his right side, hanging in a belt from his left shoulder; a plain hood about his neck, covering his shoulders, and hanging back behind him.[14]

Of course, they found him. The sun beat down on the noisy, bloody and chaotic streets of midsummer London, and the block set up the previous day in the Cheap was glutinous with the blood of Thursday's dead. As the City shuddered to the sounds of the massacre, and bodies piled up in the streets, it was here that another was added to their number, as one of London's greatest merchants lost his life to brutal decapitation.

FIFTEEN

CRISIS

> The rebels committed . . . many other enormities without sparing any
> grade or order – in churches and cemeteries, in roads and streets as
> well as in houses and fields. Neither fearing God nor revering the
> honour of mother church, they pursued and executed all those against
> whom they raised their cry. After a whole day spent in such detestable
> actions, they were at last exhausted by their labours and the drinking
> of so much more wine than usual; thus in the evening you could see
> them lying scattered about on the streets and under the walls, sleeping
> like slaughtered pigs.
>
> THOMAS WALSINGHAM

Westminster Abbey, Saturday, 15 June, 9 a.m.[1]

Richard Imworth, keeper of the King's Bench prison in Southwark,
was a jailer and a brute. He was responsible for the custody of prisoners who found themselves on the wrong side of the law, and
indicted for serious crimes against the king's peace. He was known
as 'a tormentor without pity'[2] by those who resided under his watch
in the prison down on the south bank of the Thames. He had been
a marked man from the beginning of the revolt, and when Southwark
suffered at the hands of raiders from the Blackheath camp on
Wednesday, Imworth's property and his life had been explicitly placed
under threat.

As a result, Imworth was hiding. Since the first word had reached

London that the rebels were advancing towards the City, Imworth had known that he would be one of their targets. By Saturday 15th, it may even have surprised him that he had survived the previous two days. The murders that had taken place on Corpus Christi and the following day – Legett, Sudbury, Hales, Legge, Appleton and Somenour; hundreds of foreigners and numerous overzealous agents of the law – had been visited on a group of which Imworth was quite clearly a member. An agent of the royal law renowned for his diligent, unsympathetic application to duty had every reason to fear the rebels' wrath.

The paranoia and panic that had gripped Imworth and his wife in the days immediately before the revolt had been obvious to his prisoners – indeed, one later claimed that as the rebels approached the capital in the days leading up to Corpus Christi, he had been entrusted with some small items from the Imworth family treasury to safeguard in the event of retribution from the rebels.[3] Now, on Saturday morning, seeking proximity to one of the few remaining outposts of royal authority, Imworth had taken refuge in Westminster Abbey.

The abbey should symbolically, if not militarily, have been the safest haven in the City and suburbs. It was grand, imposing, reasonably secure and intimidatingly pompous. It represented the locus of royal divinity, true in its fourteenth-century form to the magnificent design of Richard II's great-great-great-grandfather, Henry III. English kings had been crowned here since before the Norman Conquest, with ever-greater ceremony, pageantry and rhetoric concerning their bond of duty to rule. The great kings of the Plantagenet dynasty lay buried in its vaults, with pride of place going to an Anglo-Saxon: Edward the Confessor, the sainted patriarch who had ruled England with legendary holiness and laid the abbey's foundations, and to whose memory and bodily remains great miracles had been ascribed.[4]

The abbey was the place where the legal and mystical aspects of kingship came together – a place of awe and of profound sanctity. With sanctity came sanctuary, and to sully either in the abbey was taboo. As Gaunt knew from the Hawley affair, the Church took an extremely dim view of any violation committed here, and it was said that St Peter did likewise, and would severely punish transgressors on the Day of Judgement.

So, of all the churches, chapels, monastic houses and hospitals in and around London, this should have been the place, if there were one, that the rebels dared not approach. Knowing this, and knowing that the streets of the City now flowed with the blood of the hundreds massacred by the demented mob, Imworth had thrown himself upon the mercy of the Westminster monks and entrusted his person to the sanctuary of the abbey.

But if he thought that those who had shown the measure of their regard for the wrath of the Almighty and his saints by breaking out and murdering targets from churches all around the City would draw the line at entering Westminster, he was sorely mistaken. At 9 a.m. they arrived from London, beating what was now a well-trodden path.[5] The previous day, the bloody array of ministers' heads had been paraded down to the abbey, while a raiding party had also attempted to break into the treasury there, with the intention of destroying legal records.

The new morning had not much dimmed their bloodlust, and as there were now rebels well familiar with the layout of the abbey, it seems that they had little difficulty pushing their way in and making for the high altar, where Imworth cowered, perhaps hoping that the mercy he had denied others might somehow be bestowed upon him.

Imworth might have been vicious, but he was not stupid. With an instinct for the symbolism of his surroundings, he had chosen as his refuge the shrine of the Confessor. He would have banked on the first rebels to burst in immediately seeing the shrine, which stood just behind the altar, for it was visible all the way down the nave, a raised mound approached by two small steps on which pilgrims knelt in pairs, their knees polishing the stonework. He would have hoped that the sight of the shrine, flanked on either side by two pillars, one topped with a statue of the Confessor, the other with St John disguised as a pilgrim, would have brought to rebel minds the seriousness of the crime that they were about to attempt.[6]

It should have, but when the rebels did break into the abbey, their hearts proved as hard as the smooth, cold floor of the nave. As they approached, the sound of their footsteps bouncing around and up into the vaulted roof, they would have recognised Imworth clinging, literally for his life, to one of these pillars, and beside him the gold feretory containing the coffin of the Confessor. Was there an exchange of words? Did Imworth try to appeal to his kidnappers' God-fearing consciences? We do not know. All we do know is that alongside the high altar of the highest place of sanctuary in all of England, Richard Imworth, tormentor of men, was plucked from the pillar of the richly gilded shrine to England's patron saint, hauled down the nave, outside into the cool morning air and off into London, to be beheaded at Cheapside.

As the mob took Imworth up to the broad marketplace and bloodied makeshift chopping blocks of Cheapside, they chanced upon a valet named John of Greenfield, who made the grave error of 'speaking well of John of Gaunt's murdered physician William Appleton and other victims of the rebels' murderous purges'. He was seized in Bread Street, the long north–south thoroughfare that ran through the City down to the riverside port of Queenhithe, dragged north up it to the Cheap and murdered with Imworth.

By lunchtime, anarchy reigned. No law ruled now – nothing but the will of the rebels. There were no more lines to cross.

By mid-morning news would have reached the royal base at the Queen's Wardrobe and Baynard's Castle that the abbey had been desecrated. There were still reports of house-burning and widespread violence in the City. Worse, rioting was breaking out across the south-east. There were pockets of popular disturbance in Middlesex, Hertfordshire, Cambridgeshire, Norfolk and Suffolk, where the senior royal judge, Sir John Cavendish, was reported dead. Some of these were merely in sympathy for the London rebellion, but others, very worryingly, were claiming the direction and protection of Wat Tyler himself.

The day and night of chaos that had followed the Mile End conference had demonstrated the terrible error of the appeasement strategy Richard had pursued on the advice of his more timorous nobles. With the blood of his two most senior ministers and several hundred, largely innocent, inhabitants of London, Richard had bought nothing but anarchy, blasphemy, treachery, theft, extortion, arson and murder. Now he was faced with the worst threat to England's internal order in living memory.

Rumours swept through the City: Tyler was going to light fires in four corners of London and burn it to the ground; the king was going to be taken hostage; the Church was going to be abolished; John Ball was going to be the chief and only bishop in England; all other lords and bishops were going to be executed.

Attempts to negotiate with the rebel leadership via messenger were proving fruitless: in the last twenty-four hours Tyler had three times refused to accept chartered peace terms on a par with those taken by the bands that had departed from Mile End, correctly surmising that with chaos came momentum for his movement. Any rational, political character to his aims had disappeared, and a muddled vision of a society shorn of all real administrative institutions came to the fore.

Now, after days of holding back from his headstrong counsel, it seems that Richard finally started listening seriously to the advice of William Walworth. Walworth, confident in the resources he banked upon mustering through his own political and financial influence and that of his colleagues Nicholas Brembre and John Philipot, combined with the belligerent military know-how of the veteran Sir Robert Knolles, seems to have been a consistent voice favouring tough action against the rebels. He had advocated a decisive show of force against them since Thursday night; what had smacked of haughty recklessness then now seemed to be the only course of action left.

The argument against military action was fear that the loyalty of the London commons could not be relied upon, and that to provoke them into full uproar with the radical Kentishmen would spell destruction for the City. But in the light of events since Mile End, that argument was defunct. In terms of public order, there was little left to maintain, and if the latest rumours were correct, then by Monday night, Tyler planned to have the whole City burning in any case. Stopping him was therefore imperative: if they succeeded, there was a slim chance that the City could be saved; if they continued negotiations with a rebel captain whom they now had good reason to suspect was acting in bad faith, it would certainly be lost. With the terror now spreading all over the south-east and East Anglia, and word likely to be leaking out of the country to England's enemy across the Channel, the end of London could easily mean the fall of the whole realm.

So on Saturday morning, as the holiest sanctuary in his realm was being vandalised by the mob, it seems that Richard must have given his permission to mobilise the well-armed private forces of soldiers like Knolles, and the resourceful merchant oligarchs – Walworth, Brembre, Philipot and their associates. The rebels were to be drawn once again outside the City walls, this time to the closest practical point to the new royal headquarters: the great playing fields and marketplace at West Smithfield, half a mile north of Baynard's Castle and the Queen's Wardrobe, just outside Aldersgate, the north-east entrance to the City wall. Messengers were briefed to make the proclamation that Richard was coming once more to meet the rebels, and that they should all remove to Smithfield in readiness for their king.

The choice of Smithfield, rather than a return visit to Mile End, was not random. It was a logical site for negotiations with a massed band of rebels, for the fields were used to holding massive crowds on festivals and holidays, when fairs, markets and tournaments were held there. As such, it would have been familiar territory to many of the London insurgents, and probably a fair number of those rural rebels who had visited the capital for trade or festivities. In summoning his subjects there, Richard would once again have given them a sense of what we could now think of as home advantage, a placatory gesture that also no doubt played to Tyler's pride, puffed up as it was by his unpunished intransigence in the peace negotiations that had taken place so far.

If negotiations were all that were to take place at Smithfield, then this was a soothing environment in which to conduct them. It was also, however, a clever choice of venue in anticipation of Walworth's armed strategy. Smithfield was physically walled on its eastern side by the precincts of St Bartholomew's Hospital and its sister priory. To the north, a combination of the walls of the Charterhouse and the shallow waters of Faggeswell Brook provided awkward natural boundaries; while to the south-west, the deeper swells of the River Holborn and the City ditch controlled access back into London. In short, Smithfield was a welcoming but semi-enclosed environment, in which a pitched battle could be at worst contained and in the best case turned – even by a modest military force – into a rout. There was the whiff of bold, ruthless and calculating strategic planning behind the Smithfield meeting. Whether it would prove necessary to negotiate with the sword would be up to the character of the young king. And that, as had been proven by Mile End, was the great unknown.

Richard himself, in anticipation of the most critical moment of his short life and shorter reign, gathered together his large retinue of nobles, knights and attendants, and set out on what might have been a final pilgrimage. Before he could once again meet his delinquent subjects, he needed to seek spiritual solace, and ask the favour of God for what he was about to face. So, following in the footsteps of the mob, Richard set out for Westminster and the shrine of the Confessor.

SIXTEEN

SMITHFIELD

When the king with his retinue arrived there, he turned to the east
... and the commons arrayed themselves in bands of great size on
the west side ... And when he was called by the mayor, this chief-
tain, Wat Tyler ... approached the king with great confidence,
mounted on a little horse so that the commons might see him ...
Thereupon the said Wat rehearsed the points which were to be
demanded; and he asked that there should be no law except for the
law of Winchester ...

Anonimalle Chronicle

Smithfield, Saturday, 15 June, 5 p.m.
The sun was settling low in the sky over Smithfield; the Smooth
Field, field of meetings, place of death. Crowds streamed out of the
Newgate and Aldersgate, filing north towards London's ancient site
of horse trading and racing, games, festivals, markets and fairs.
Smithfield was a mixing ground for the rich and the humble, a playground for horse-fanciers and jockeys, tool-makers, stallholders and
farmers driving plump-uddered cows and long-flanked, snuffling
swine.[1]

It was a place where livestock was slaughtered and traitors were
butchered, where in 1305 the Scottish rebel William Wallace had
been dragged naked at the heels of a horse, strangled, castrated and
gutted, his bowels burned before him and his decapitated body

141

hacked into four parts for dispatch about the realm. Like all places of regular public gathering, Smithfield brought together the local community to mingle, trade, marvel at the tilts of knights and look on at awful, bloody punishment. Wallace was not the first to be seen off in gruesome fashion there, and the thicket of elm trees clustered in the north-west corner of the field beyond the Horse Pool watering pond had held beneath their shade many rough and gory acts of justice over the centuries.

Now, as Saturday afternoon wound towards an evening that capped a second day of anarchy in the City, masses of rebels began to arrive at Smithfield. Fanning out across the broad field towards the elms and the broken countryside to the west, they could quite easily have seen smoke still rising to the north from the Priory of St John of Jerusalem, the ruined home of the dead treasurer. Half a mile south of Smithfield was the battered Temple, ransacked on Thursday for its legal records. Back inside the City walls to the south-east lay the exhaling wrecks of houses torn down or smoked out, their inhabitants chased, threatened, harassed, intimidated, robbed, bullied or killed by the bands that had lost their discipline and their leadership, and had wallowed gluttonously in the lawlessness that had followed Richard's timid showing at Mile End. The perpetrators of these deeds spread themselves about the field, properly ordered for the first time since they had camped on Blackheath, into large organised bands.[2]

Richard approached Smithfield from Westminster, accompanied by 200 retainers. Depleted as he was, and ranked against – at the very least – several thousand rebels, his train must still have cut an impressive sight, the rich-clothed splendour of a royal party in marked contrast to the filth, soot and sweat of a woollen-clad rebel band, many of whom had spent more than a fortnight on the road. Close also to the king in spirit and probably in physical placement were Walworth and his trusted mercantile allies Philipot and Brembre.

They had all spent the afternoon in preparation for whatever was to come at Smithfield, but Walworth and Richard had gone about it in very different ways. At 3 p.m. Richard had ridden with his grand retinue out from Baynard's Castle and the Wardrobe and on to Westminster. He left his mother behind him at La Reol. Word was sent ahead to the dazed religious community of Westminster that in the light of the horror of Imworth's murder, the king would be visiting.

Shortly after passing through the village of Charing, Richard was met by a forward party of canons and vicars from the Collegiate Church of St Stephen. They arrived in a solemn procession, mantled all about in their copes, their feet bare against the cold earth. They accompanied the king back along the road to Westminster and up to the doors of the desecrated abbey.

At the abbey, Richard had dismounted from his horse, and knelt before a cross that had been carried out to him. He was brought to the shrine of St Edward, where he knelt on the smooth pilgrims' steps, tears rolling down his cheeks as he prayed devoutly to the Confessor for protection. Behind him, all of the knights and esquires in his retinue had engaged in similarly devout genuflections, weeping openly, while subtly jostling for position in the effort to appear the most pious and eager to make an offering to the saint's remains.

Richard left his own offering, then made his way out to the anchorage in the abbey garden. A hermit had lived in these grounds for some time, and Richard had repaired to this mystic man to make his confession and remain for a time in spiritual consultation.

This, then, was the pious young king's preparation for the greatest test of his life.

Mayor Walworth had more pragmatic concerns. Before he left the City he had fitted himself with body armour beneath his fine clothes. He had then made sure that all those servants of the king who had access to and command of men and weapons were ready to act on his word. He must have advised London's aldermen to be ready to join him in defending the City. While all at Westminster made their offerings to the shrine, Walworth's mind would have been occupied with the likelihood that soon he would be called upon to raise arms to protect the City that had made his name and fortune.

When Richard emerged from the garden, his soul refreshed from his conversation with the anchorite, the royal party set out for Smithfield. The rebels were always noisy, and their clamouring would have carried through the afternoon's stillness as the royal retinue closed in on the meeting place.

The party turned east when they arrived at Smithfield, keeping their distance from the bloc of rebels arrayed to the west, and stopped in front of the Priory of St Bartholomew. The huge, thickset Norman church of St Bartholomew-the-Great loomed behind them, while the massed ranks of the most troublesome popular army ever to be raised in England waited restlessly across the field to the north-west.[3]

Walworth, beside the king, was ready. So was Richard. He called the mayor close and asked him to ride out to the ranked masses and demand that Tyler approach.

Walworth had been eye to eye with Tyler before, staring across London Bridge two days earlier as the Kentish general directed the terror unleashed on Southwark and organised the storming of the bridge. Now the gap between these two rough-hewn leaders was not the swirling eddies of the Thames, but the smooth turf of Smithfield, bitten here and there by hoof-prints, dried piles of dung erupting from its surface like molehills. The mayor rode out to the rebels, stopped his horse before them and called for Tyler by name, summoning the chief author of all the weekend's misery to show himself before the king.[4] Then he wheeled around and returned to Richard's side.

As Walworth stood before Tyler's ranks and bellowed the leader's name, Tyler himself must have been filled with pride and self-importance. Not in his fondest imagination could he have predicted such a moment as this: the mayor of London summoning him, the general of an army of the shires, to come before the king. It was validation – elevation, even – the stuff of outlaw ballads and popular legend.[5]

The royal retinue was set back a safe distance from the rebel ranks, and Tyler rode out towards it filled with supreme confidence. Thus far the rebels had triumphed in all their interactions with agents of the Crown. Whether outnumbering them in destructive rioting, outmanoeuvring them in negotiations or simply chopping off their heads and putting them on poles, Tyler and his fellow rebel leaders had shown themselves to be irresistible generals and persuasive demagogues. Tyler knew it. But he also knew that the key to all that had gone before in the revolt had been skilful management of popular momentum. From the early days in the villages to the massacres about the City, everything had been bound together by the fervent belief that still greater successes lay around the corner.

For that reason, Tyler trotted his horse out in the direction of Walworth's retreat ready to present the king with a set of populist demands that would go far beyond the pragmatic, and frame the revolt in the language of social revolution. He had in mind a scheme of requests that far exceeded the modest political demands of Mile End, which would entail the total transformation of society from the lawyer- and landowner-dominated state it now was, and back to the fabled shire community they imagined their great-grandfathers had known 100 years before.

As the limber and roll of his horse carried him step by inevitable step closer to his king, Tyler's mind filled with the scope of what he had decided to ask. When he drew up before the royal party, he seems to have been half delirious.

The late afternoon sun slanted down on his woollen hood, but he did not take it off. To do so would have felt like deference. Nor did he dismount from his horse, until he was sure that the commons assembled on the far side of the field could see him in front of the king. He felt the blunt press of his dagger handle in his side, and slipped it out into his hand. With the other, he kept his balance as he dismounted from the little horse.

Richard looked at this peculiar sight, and saw a rough, arrogant and self-conscious older man clamber one-handed from his mount, armed and giddy with pride. In a hopeless and unwitting parody of his betters, the rebel captain half-curtsied at Richard, then lunged forward, grabbing his arm and shaking it roughly in comradely greeting.

'Brother, be of good comfort and joyful,' rasped Tyler, 'for you shall have, in the fortnight that is to come, forty thousand more commons than you have at present, and we shall be good companions.'[6]

Good companions? Even ignoring the crude attempt to intimidate him, Richard can scarcely have heard anything so impudent in his life. It certainly riled those around the king, and the mood immediately tautened.

Richard asked Tyler: 'Why will you not go back to your own country?'

Perhaps irritated by the child's dismissive lack of comradely respect, Tyler swore a great oath, saying that neither he nor the masses ranked away on the side of the Horse Pool would leave until they had a charter as they had demanded. This was a petulant demand, and Tyler followed it with another ugly threat – if his demands were not met, the lords of the realm would rue it bitterly.

Hackles must have been raised on the royal side. But Richard remained calm, seemingly unwilling to countenance head-on confrontation. Just as at Mile End, he tried to call the rebels' bluff, asking Tyler for his demands, and saying that whatever he demanded, he should have, freely, and written out under the royal seal. Even after the events that followed Mile End, Richard was still prepared to pursue the line of least resistance as a means to taking the sting out of Tyler's populist campaign. At Mile End he had probably known he was gambling with the lives of his ministers in the Tower – now he had reason to believe he was risking the fate of London and possibly his Crown. Perhaps with the rebels lined up, armed, organised and outnumbering the royal party by hundreds to one, there was little other option.

This played nicely to Tyler's arrogance. Sensing his moment, he began to speak. What emerged was less a list of demands than a fantastical description of the shire community. It was an ideal of England rooted in popular tradition. Gone were the specific political demands of Mile End, and in their place was a song of freedom – a paean to a wished-for world, a giant village community with a simple, popular law: the law of Winchester.

Winchester was the old Anglo-Saxon capital of England, burial place of the British kings such as Alfred, birthplace of the Domesday Book (also known as *Liber Wintoniensis*, or the Book of Winchester), which many villagers believed held the secrets of their ancient rights of landholding. The town was closely associated with Edward I, whose Statute of Winchester in 1285 had codified community policing, and called for all villagers to share in the responsibility of keeping the peace, as opposed to central agents of the law, who were seen as having patchy knowledge of and little regard for local community. It sanctioned unsparing punishment for all criminals ('no one will be spared and no felony will be concealed'), a sentiment that clearly resonated with the vengeful rebels so rampant in the aftermath of Mile End. Winchester was the home of ancient, traditional, moral law, and of government rooted in divine equity and a love for the simple principles of right and wrong that were assumed to be the true measure of good kingship.

As Tyler began to elaborate his philosophy, it became clear how far from reality the rebel vision had strayed. The end to serfdom that had been demanded at Mile End had now blossomed into a demand for the end of lordship wholesale. There should be no more outlawry, and no lordship of any sort, except for that of the king. Tyler called for the abolition of the Church hierarchy, and the appointment of only one bishop and one prelate. All clerical lands and possessions not required to provide an adequate living to their owners should be stripped from the Church and divided among the people of the parish. Finally, Tyler repeated the Mile End demand for an end to villeinage, declaring that all men in England ought to be free and of the same condition.

With this final, thunderous vision painted thickly in the rich colours of his spiritual comrade John Ball, Tyler closed his speech.

What could Richard reply? This was not a negotiating position. It was the fantasy of a madman. But after the weekend just passed, that was hardly a surprise.

Sticking to his chosen policy of appeasing the rebels by any means possible, the young king told Tyler that he could have whatever he could fairly grant, 'reserving only for himself the regality of his Crown'.

Then, rather more sharply, he told Tyler to go home.

SEVENTEEN

SHOWDOWN

> ... on this, the king, although a boy and of tender age, took courage
> and ordered the mayor of London to arrest Tyler. The mayor ...
> arrested Tyler without question and struck him a blow on the head
> which hurt him badly ... His death, as he fell from his horse to the
> ground, was the first incident to restore to the English knighthood
> their almost extinct hope that they could resist the commons.
> Immediately the commons saw Tyler's downfall they cried with sorrow
> for his death: 'Our captain is dead; our leader has been treacherously
> killed. Let us stay together and die with him; let us fire our arrows
> and staunchly avenge his death.' And so they drew their bows and
> prepared to shoot ...
>
> THOMAS WALSINGHAM

Smithfield, Saturday, 15 June, 6 p.m.

There was silence.

Wat Tyler and Richard II stood face to face, each uncertain what
to do next. Tyler's demand for a vision of England with the clock
turned back to a semi-imaginary time of ancient traditions and a
lordless society had met with the one response that did not suit him:
complete acquiescence.

Part of the point of asking for such radical terms of peace had
been to maintain the momentum of the revolt, which now seemed
to be spreading into East Anglia, and drawing in ever-greater numbers

of rebels. Pursuing these sorts of demands kept the movement vital, idealistic and committed. But without such a central focus, it would inevitably dissolve back into local riots and isolated spates of rural complaint. Royal assent to his ludicrous demands guaranteed Tyler nothing.

Richard seemed to have realised this, and was prepared to repeat the monumental gamble of Mile End even with now the entire safety of his capital city at stake. If he lost, then the rumours of Tyler's intention to torch the whole City and murder every noble and churchman inside it stood to be realised. But if he won, he stood to gain everything. He faced down Tyler, his retinue silent behind him, and his heart presumably jumping almost clean out of his chest. To every other party to this stand-off, the impasse between Richard and Tyler was so unbearably tense that they hesitated to say a single word, for fear of provoking some egregious act of violence. The two men stared at each other in silence, neither willing to back down.

Tyler broke first. The heat of the moment and of the summer afternoon must suddenly have felt very oppressive. In an attempt to earn himself some physical respite, he turned and demanded a jug of water. When it arrived, he swilled it around his mouth deliberately coarsely and spat in front of the king; an act of gross vulgarity before his lord. Then he demanded a jug of ale. Again, this was brought, and Tyler took another great slug from it, before climbing – without having been given leave to depart the king's presence – back on to his horse.

It was clear from his disrespect that Tyler had completely lost his grip on reality. His ambition now stretched beyond reform and restitution. The power he had wielded for the last week had totally consumed him, and the way he acted towards Richard suggests that he truly believed that before long the whole realm would bend to his will as king of the commons. Tiring of the negotiations, and having shown his contempt for his opponents with his deliberate show of bad manners, he made as if to leave.

What occurred next happened quickly. Tyler's display of baseness and blatant disrespect for his king's worship had exceeded the patience of Richard's servants. A mocking cry went up from among the royal retinue to the effect that the rebel leader was nothing more than a common thief and a robber. Some later said it came from Sir John Newton, Tyler's hostage from Blackheath – others that it was merely a valet from Richard's party. Either way, the words rankled with Tyler, and he took the bait, gripping his dagger and retorting angrily that whoever had just spoken would lose his head.

This was the moment that Walworth had been waiting for. The mayor rode out to Tyler – who was waving his dagger and ranting – and shouted that he was arresting him for his contemptible behaviour in the king's presence. But as he made a grab for the rebel leader, Tyler thrust at him with his dagger, aiming to cut through his vital organs.

The blow bounced off Walworth's body armour, and with that single, blunt collision of blade on vest, Tyler was doomed. Walworth, triumphant, pulled out his own dagger – a short blade known as a baselard – and plunged it deep into Tyler's neck. Then he pulled it out and thrust it again, this time hitting Tyler's head. The exchange of blows happened in a flash – but there were others who were as alert as Walworth. A royal valet, Sir Ralph Standish, broke ranks and hurtled towards the grappling men, running the rebel leader through with a sword.

From the other side of Smithfield, with the shadows of the elm trees lengthening across the field towards St Bartholomew's, the rebel army could neither hear nor understand any of this. All they saw was a period of brief animation between their leader and a couple of figures from the royal party, all of them on horseback. Then they saw Tyler wheel away, spurring his horse towards them.

They did not see the blood pouring from his neck; nor could they make out his dying cries for revenge. They just saw the skittish dance of his small horse towards them and, then, after he had come 80 yards, their leader – who had brought them from Maidstone to London, who had unleashed them in the City, and now represented them before the king – fall like a rag doll from his horse and collapse to the ground.

There was bewilderment, then anger. What had happened? The silent tableau offered them nothing. What had been said on the other side of the field? What was the message that Tyler had been bringing? Why had he fallen, when he was apparently charging vigorously back towards them? Their only reaction was to bend back the strings of their bows, and ready themselves to fire.

On the royal side, similar confusion reigned. The king's party had the advantage of knowing that the mayor had felled Tyler, but Walworth had turned his own horse and charged away from the scene the instant that he had withdrawn his knife from Tyler's head. That spooked the king's ranks, and several of the knights and squires of the household began to panic and followed Walworth's charge back to London.

For the boy who had hitherto seemed so timid and passive in the jaws of crisis, Richard's next act was remarkable. He drew on the strength he had garnered that afternoon at St Edward's tomb, his own instinct of faith in the rebel protestations of loyalty to him alone, and the spirit of the moment; and for the first time in his reign, Richard acted decisively and bravely. He kicked his own horse forward, racing past Tyler's fallen body and on towards the rebels. As he approached he began to shout to them that he commanded them as their king to make their way out of Smithfield and follow him to Clerkenwell Fields, a safer, more open space a few hundred yards to the north.

To the rebels, this swift turnaround must have seemed almost like a dream. They were wrongfooted by the speed with which Tyler had fallen, and the confusing movement among the royal party across the field, but before they descended into anarchy, Richard had stepped in. To their eyes Richard was fulfilling the role of the kings of legend, the benevolent leader recognising his true subjects, seeing their audacious behaviour as a defence of justice. A seemingly trance-like spirit took hold of the whole company. Spellbound by the sight of their teenage king, they lowered their weapons and began to follow him across the field, like sheep.

To Richard – riding at the head of a ragtag mob of several

thousand of his lowly subjects – it must have seemed utterly surreal. He had never seen his father or grandfather in their full glory, leading troops into the battlefield. It was to his credit that he went along with the momentum that had turned in his favour, but it must also have been an exhilarating feeling for him – and as he rode, a whole vision of his own kingship was confirmed in his young mind.

He led the rebels purposefully out of Smithfield to the open fields at Clerkenwell. Here the strange army settled, Richard at the head, and the rank-and-file arrayed in their bands on the western side.

Meanwhile, Walworth rode hard back to London, Tyler's blood drying on the dagger by his side. He would have hoped, as he tore towards the Aldersgate, that his instructions to the loyal soldiers of the City and the aldermen who controlled the musters in the twenty-four London wards would carry, and that the citzens' nerve would hold. He had probably used Brembre and Philipot to enforce his message in the wards, but having seen the royal guards at the Tower suffer a collective failure of nerve two days earlier, raising London in force against the rebels required faith in the willingness of the citizens to save their City.

That faith was repaid. Ward by ward, the citizens that had remained in the City armed themselves and headed to Smithfield and Richard's aid. Sir Robert Knolles led a company of knights, whom he had kept in reserve during all the previous days of the revolt.[1] Other companies of armed citizens followed behind. Walworth sent them off in their numbers, the aldermen leading the keepers of the wards, a well-armed parade finally ready to throw themselves against their enemies in defence of their livelihoods. But the mayor himself hung back to collect a company of lances. His most important business remained unfinished.

The last thing that Walworth had seen as he charged back to London was Tyler, wounded but defiant, charging towards his men with vengeance on his lips. The mayor knew that destroying the captain once and for all was vital if the rebels were to be dispersed. He rode, determined, towards Smithfield, ready to separate the ailing Tyler from his allies and finish him off.

When Walworth arrived back at Smithfield, he found it empty. Neither the rebels nor the king were there. Looking north, he could see the rebel army hemmed in on all sides by the aldermen and citizens – he would have to trust that the king was safe now in the hands of the reinforcements.

But where was Tyler?

A brief enquiry revealed that he had been taken, alive but fatally wounded, to the hospital of St Bartholomew, yards from where he was struck down. Walworth went to the hospital, where the rebel captain languished in bed, half dead and at the mercy of the master. Walworth had Tyler dragged from his deathbed, and hauled, bleeding, to the middle of Smithfield. Those few companions who had remained with their sad captain were forced to watch as he was propped up in the field and beheaded.[2]

Across in Clerkenwell Field, an uneasy stand-off was taking place. The rebels had temporarily surrendered themselves to Richard's leadership, but the speed with which Walworth's muster had arrived had taken them by surprise. Now they were penned in on all sides by a better-equipped, better-drilled force, and deprived of their inspirational general, the last sighting of whom had been his limp body being carted away in the direction of the hospital.

The presence of the king was the only encouraging sign, for all the signals he had given them thus far were that he would act benevolently towards his loyal subjects. But that illusion was halted suddenly, as the judder of hoofs on the soil announced the arrival of Mayor Walworth.

He bore a grisly relic. Wat Tyler's head, hoodless but easily recognised, was carried in front of the company of lancers, just as Archbishop Sudbury's head had been paraded down to Westminster some days previously. The king summoned the pole-bearer, and had Tyler's head set up in front of him, to symbolise that the rebellion was finished, its captain defeated and the City saved. Ignoring the rebels, he thanked the mayor effusively for what he had done.

Seeing this was too much for the exhausted commons. Their will to fight drained away, and they sank to their knees among the corn-rows of Clerkenwell, beaten in arms and broken in spirit. Cries for mercy went up, imploring the king to show forgiveness and let them go home. There was nothing for Richard to prove, and he was not foolhardy enough to provoke any more violence that weekend. He appointed two knights to lead the way through London, and sent the rebels packing.

As they watched the men file out of the field, guarded on all sides by the quickly assembled citizen army, Richard turned to Walworth and told him to put a basinet on his head. A basinet was a small, pointed metal helmet designed to protect the head in battle, and Walworth was understandably confused. With all signs of danger passed, he asked the king why he now needed protection.

Richard told him that as repayment for the great debt he owed Walworth for saving the City, he was going to knight him in the field, and that he ought to look fit for his new station. After a few token protestations, Walworth kneeled and, with Brembre, Philipot and Robert Launde alongside him, all four men received the firm dubbing of knights of the realm.

With this honourable scene playing out behind them, the rebel army filed away from Clerkenwell, tired men casting long shadows in the late light of a dying day. They were shepherded back through the subdued City, through the large gates in the north wall, then south through the narrow streets and thoroughfares such as Bread Street, back towards Bridge Ward. The streets were no longer theirs. The executioners' blocks at Cheapside were now nothing but monu-ments to a festival that had come to an end: an orgy of retribution that had thrashed itself to a bloody conclusion. The Tower, so recently the rebels' playground, now loomed ominous, as the shroud of the summer twilight closed around it. Down at the river, where Flemish blood had darkened the eddies of the Thames, the drawbridge was lowered, and the Kent rebels passed in a sad parade back out of the City the same way they had come.

They knew the road home backwards.

PART III

EIGHTEEN

RETRIBUTION

> The king to his beloved and faithful William of Walworth . . . greetings. We desire with all our heart, especially at this time of disturbance, to duly protect, save and securely rule the city of London in the face of the invasion of those men who (as you know) have recently risen . . . We assign, appoint and ordain you . . . to keep, defend, protect, rule and govern the said city, its suburbs and other places without . . . at our command but according to your own discretion . . . you are to punish everyone who makes or presumes to make riots, risings and assemblies against our peace . . . either according to the law of our kingdom of England or by other ways and methods, by beheading and the mutilation of limbs, as seems to you most expeditious and sensible . . .
>
> Royal Commission issued after Smithfield

Saturday, 15–Sunday, 16 June

Through the coincidence of divine providence and mayoral pragmatism, London had been saved. The pallid young king could have picked no more dramatic moment to come of age, while Walworth, the hard-bitten, wealthy old fishmonger who had plucked the City from the flames of the furious mob, had proven that he was a man of level-headed action.

As Sir William Walworth, Sir John Philipot, Sir Nicholas Brembre and Sir Robert Launde rose from being dubbed knights on the hard turf of Clerkenwell, there can only have been relief at God's grace in delivering them from such severe adversity. The Kent rebels who trooped beaten and bewildered back through London could so easily have been swarming back in like a returning plague to finish the capital once and for all.

But the victory that Richard and his circle of loyal Londoners had won was by no means final. True, after the muddle of Mile End the flow of rebels to London had reversed, with tired villagers making their way back home with their charters of emancipation. But ripples of violent disaffection travelled with them.

The tremors of unrest rumbled out from London to the outlying towns and villages of the south-east, East Anglia and beyond with remarkable speed. While London had been the focus of the most dramatic uproar, by the time of the Smithfield confrontation, almost all of the southern counties had experienced some form of disruption. Trouble had flared continuously in Essex and Kent; villages in Middlesex and Surrey were in turmoil at the same time as London.

There was early trouble at the manor of St Albans in Hertfordshire, observed and recorded in scandalised detail by the resident chronicler there, Thomas Walsingham. The townsfolk had risen against the rule of the abbot of St Albans, Thomas de la Mare, and marched on London on the day of the Mile End meeting. Now, as word spread that London had been allowed to boil for three full days, with precious little resistance from the government, the spirit of disobedience and topsy-turvy threatened to carry throughout the entire realm.

Smithfield excepted, there had been precious little decisive action from the Crown. The state of torpor and paralysis could no longer be allowed to continue. Now, spurred into action, Richard gave his consent for the first strong move to restore order. Back in the City, with night now fallen, a royal commission was drawn up, conferring remarkable powers on the mayor and his allies. Walworth, Brembre, Philipot, Launde and their capable military ally Sir Robert Knolles were jointly appointed to an extraordinary panel with powers to hunt out, try and punish rebels wherever they found them. That did not just mean London. Assisted by the noted lawyers Sir Robert

Belknap and William Cheyne, they were permitted, in theory, to carry out their investigations anywhere within a 70-mile radius of the City – throughout Essex, Kent, Sussex, Surrey and Middlesex.

This was unusual, to say the least. Though the new Clerkenwell knights had all served as senior London aldermen, and Walworth, Philipot and Brembre had been in control of parliamentary war finance for a short while in the 1370s, raising them to the position of cross-county hanging judges unconstrained by any of the normal conventions of the common law was a bold move. But if anything had been demonstrated by the rebels' assaults on the City, it was the necessity of firm, pitiless action.

Richard effectively devolved the whole business of emergency government to this committee of seven men. They were appointed to 'keep, defend, protect, rule and govern the said city, its suburbs and other places without, both by sea and by water, at our command but according to your discretion, by the means which seem to you most safe and expedient'.[1] They were granted the power to command the defence of the city and the areas around it, to hunt out any illegal assemblies and pacify them as they saw fit.

Walworth's commission was given explicit command over the entire network of royal law in the shires and towns around London – sheriffs, aldermen, citizen juries and all – and it was awarded awful powers of retribution. Those who made 'riots, risings and assemblies against the peace' were to be punished 'either according to the law of our kingdom of England or by other ways and methods, by beheadings and mutilation of limbs, as seems to you most expeditious and sensible . . .'

These punishments went way beyond what was prescribed by law for even the worst treachery during ordinary times. Hanging usually punished felony, with traitors drawn as an aggravating discomfort. Beheading and mutilation spoke of anger, and it is possible for perhaps the first time to detect the young hand of the king – who witnessed the document in person – behind the savage instructions. He had been profoundly affected by his recent lonely days spent in the Tower. He had followed the debate between ineffectual older men professing to act in his best interests but recommending inertia while the City burned around them. His mother had been threatened, and the beloved abbey at Westminster, the site of his coronation, was desecrated by monsters. Several people to whom he was close had been savagely slaughtered. No wonder he placed his faith now in the senior citizens of London: what they lacked in nobility, they made up for in vigour.

But the orders also smacked of innate Plantagenet vindictiveness, an unpleasant trait shared by generations of Richard's ancestors. Richard must have thought of how his uncle John of Gaunt would react in his place: Gaunt, who would taunt and bully and drag his opponents about by their hair when he was slighted, and who would surely be encouraging revenge were he not still stranded far in the north. Vindictive as it was, this was a classic Plantagenet call to arms; the mark of a young man putting his stamp on government for the very first time. The next day Walworth began his duties in earnest.

As London and its suburbs awaited Walworth's wrath, the clamour of revolt in the surrounding counties began to rise. There were very likely those among the Kentish rebels who had fought in the wars with France, and they knew that the protocol for soldiers after the official end of hostilities was generally to engage in a profitable round of looting. As soon as the Smithfield meeting was dispersed, bands of rebels returning home from London began extorting money from villages like Clandon, a few miles from the City.

Up in St Albans, disturbances had been under way for some time.[2] The townsfolk had marched to London in the early morning of Friday, 14 June, passing Jack Straw's burning manor of Highbury on their way. They had been in and around the City during the Mile End conference before making their way to the Church of St Mary Arches (St Mary-le-Bow), the Norman church just south of Cheapside.

In St Mary Arches they had held a reasoned conference about the best way to go about securing their liberties from the manorial laws and customs imposed on them by the abbot. At this stage their aims had been broad ranging, but prosaic: they wanted to redefine the boundaries of the town, which affected their right to pasture their animals; to dispute and redefine fishing, hunting, fowling rights, and the rules governing hand mills and bailiffs – immediate, specific demands concerning their daily life, and requests for rights they felt had been gradually eroded since the imaginary good old days of King Henry I.

The St Albans rebels' aims were banal, and their philosophy surprisingly conservative. The hotheads among them wanted to threaten the monks with arson and murder at the hands of Tyler's ruffians, but the more level headed advocated applying to the king for a charter instructing the abbot to restore their liberties. They were angry and impassioned, but reasonable with it. At this stage, even surrounded by a City descending into chaos, this was, by and large, a group making the most of the upside-down state of society to force their hand.

But by the weekend St Albans was slipping into anarchy.

William Grindcobbe, an intemperate man with a history of assaults on monks and excommunication, had taken leadership of the townsfolk and represented them at Mile End, where he had obtained a charter of legal rights from the king. But Grindcobbe had subsequently gone to Wat Tyler, asking for reinforcements with which to threaten the abbot and ensure the terms of royal manumission. The radical, visionary mood of Tyler and his Kent rebels was infectious, and Grindcobbe had come away far more impressed by their bombast than with Richard's legal concessions. He returned to St Albans with a promise of an army of 20,000 men, to come and slay the monastic population, and a head swollen with ideas about the universal abolition of lordship.

By late afternoon on Friday, word of the brutal murders on Tower Hill had reached Hertfordshire, prompting a number of the holy men to flee for St Albans' daughter house in Northumberland. They went not a moment too soon – because when Grindcobbe and a baker called William Cadyndon returned, they declared themselves great lords and began to lead the townsfolk on a series of night raids to smash houses, woods and gates belonging to the monastery.

By Saturday, vandalism and destruction had become utterly wide-spread, large groups of rebels had descended on the town from nearby villages, and oaths of undying fealty had been sworn. The conventions of rebellion that had been observed in London were now applied to St Albans, as Grindcobbe's rebels made a conscious effort to identify themselves through their actions with the wild philosophy of Tyler's radicals. The protests about specific grievances had rapidly mutated into staged violence, which demonstrated not just their legitimate grievances against the abbot, but sang to the world of their righteous dissatisfaction with the whole social order. Another bloody summer game had begun.

All Saturday afternoon gangs of rebels from the lower ranks of St Albans society, joined by townsfolk from nearby Barnet, rampaged around the town and abbey lands. The violence they committed was, as in London, a combination of the symbolic smashing of anything that represented lordly authority, and vandalism of property that just seemed ripe for destruction. They shattered the great millstones that had been laid in the abbey cloister in the 1330s as a memento of the abbey's overlordship in the town and surrounding country-side, and handed out fragments of the stone in imitation of the distribution of bread in parish churches after the mass. They extorted all the abbot's charters of legal tenure and burned them in a great public bonfire. Then they began demanding that the abbot return to them a (mythical) charter granted by the Saxon king Offa, in which all their ancient liberties and rights were written down in beautiful letters of gold and azure.

To show their solidarity with the Londoners, the St Albans rebels had taken to imitating the chilling howls that had rung around Tower Hill as Sudbury's head had been hacked off. The abbey jail was broken open, and a prisoner dragged out to be beheaded on a large piece of land before the abbey gates. Naturally, the victim's head went up on a pole. By Saturday night, as Walworth's committee was preparing to bring order to London, St Albans and all the Hertfordshire countryside around it were already deep into their own rebellion.

Just as in London, there was a growing strain of shire conservatism behind the mayhem. While recent manorial charters were burned, and royal charters arriving from Mile End were embraced, the desire for the fabled Offa's charter grew stronger by the hour. To the rebels it became the physical symbol of their longed-for return to ancient times. The problem was that in reality it was as imaginary as the times themselves. By Sunday morning, the monks were in despair, for the rebels were threatening to burn down the monastery if Offa's charter were not returned to them. No amount of pleading from the abbot could persuade Grindcobbe's men that it did not exist. Like the king at Mile End, the abbot had diplomatically agreed to every rebel demand that addressed the reality of government, even where the result was to sanction destruction of property. But faced by the rebels' demands for physical proofs of their mystic traditions, he was as helpless as if they had asked him to saddle them a unicorn.

On Sunday morning, with the magnificent abbey threatened with burning to the ground, the monks were preparing to flee their impossible tormentors. The mob now included common men from the surrounding settlements of Luton, Watford, Barnet, Rickmansworth, Tring and Redbourn, some of whom had bullied and threatened local gentlemen into speaking on their behalf. Swathes of men milled, armed, around St Albans, revelling in their newly elevated positions and enjoying the prospect of extracting charters new and ancient from the beleaguered abbot.

The situation was saved by the rumours spreading constantly and ever more urgently from London that Wat Tyler was dead. Hot on the back of the news, rapidly spreading, that Tyler had been killed in the king's presence came a charter of protection from Richard.

That took some of the steam out of the rebellion. Grindcobbe and his fellow leaders continued to act in the high and pompous lordly fashion which they had adopted in the previous days, but they tempered it with a greater sense of decorum in their negotiations – the roads around the abbey were no longer blocked, and there seemed, suddenly, to be a chance of saving the monastery from the mob.

Negotiations continued on Sunday, in a more civilised fashion, though with Abbot de la Mare presumably grinding his teeth at the presumption and arrogance of the rebels. For the next few days nearby villagers continued to arrive at the abbey, trampling around the grounds waving rusty axes and making demands for liberties, the restoration of old customs and freedom from labour service. But they did so with ever-decreasing conviction, and none of the hotheadedness that had infected Saturday's events.

Back in London, word had filtered through of the abbey's predicament. Richard had followed his appointment of Walworth's punitive commission by appointing the steward of the royal household, Sir Hugh Segrave, as Keeper of the Great Seal. But the best that Segrave and his fellow knight Sir Thomas Percy, who was a benefactor of St Albans, could do was to write to the abbot, advising him to continue to agree to all of the rebels' demands until royal assistance could be sent.

Segrave, Percy and the regrouped royal council would have been very troubled that the influence and spirit of Tyler's movement had passed so quickly north. But the news of the chaos at St Albans was swiftly becoming just one skein in a web of disorder being spun at speed outwards from London. By the end of Sunday, disturbances were spiralling out of control across Buckinghamshire, Bedfordshire, Cambridgeshire, Norfolk and Suffolk; urban disorder had reached as far north as Beverley, in Yorkshire. Essex remained turbulent, and Kent also had the potential to erupt back into revolt.

And though Tyler was dead, new leaders were beginning to come to prominence: names such as William Grindcobbe, John Wrawe and Geoffrey Litster were beginning to promise serious danger as they led bands of rebels on other outposts of lordly authority. And somewhere in all of this remained the most elusive and dangerous demagogue of them all: John Ball.

NINETEEN

THE BISHOP

In Essex, Suffolk and Norfolk, the commons ... rose in large numbers
at various places, did many wrongs and beheaded many worthy men
... They beheaded John Cavendish, chief justice of the king, and also
executed Sir Robert Salle ... Likewise at Peterborough the neighbours
and tenants of the abbot rose against him and proposed to kill him,
which they would have done without redress had God not laid his
restraining hand upon them at the last moment. For help came in
the shape of lord Henry le Spencer, bishop of Norwich ...

HENRY KNIGHTON

Monday, 17 June

John Ball was on the run.

After Smithfield, he headed north. Unlike the rebel rank-and-file,
Ball could not return to Kent or Essex – even before the revolt he
had been notorious in those counties, and now, having preached to
tens of thousands at Blackheath, and been party to the murder of
an archbishop at Tower Hill, he was one of the best-known men in
south-east England.

As Ball moved north, heading in the direction of York, his birthplace, news raced ahead of him. Word of the rebellion he had baptised
with his rhetoric had now spread to his home town. Even as he
travelled on Monday, aggrieved townsmen had begun destroying
York's gates, walls and religious houses.

York was among the most northerly points of what was now fast becoming a national insurrection. Scarborough and Beverley, too, were facing insurrection. Latent tensions in towns and communities all the way up the east coast and inland as far as Leicester and Buckinghamshire were set to flame by news of what had happened in London. Ball was travelling in harness with the sweep of anarchy.[1]

It seems likely that he moved close to the western border of the insurgency, without ever straying deep into its new heartlands. With the government slowly moving into action to try to provide some sort of resistance, it would have been too dangerous. Preaching, too, would have exposed him, but this put Ball in a dilemma: how could he retain influence over a movement he felt he owned without making himself vulnerable to arrest and the same fate that had already befallen his comrade Tyler?

The answer lay in finding a new means of spreading his message, so as he travelled he wrote letters of spiritual instruction, and began to send them out to his distant flock. Numerous examples of Ball's letters survive, and they are a compelling insight into his state of mind. He saw both the ideals of the movement diluted and its true adherents wavering in the face of the loss at Smithfield and the easy resort to simple plunder. As revealed in his words, Ball's concerns about the changing nature of his revolt could not have been plainer. One typical letter went to the Essex contingent:

John Schep, sometime Saint Mary priest of York, and now of Colchester, greeteth well John Nameless and John the Miller, and John Carter, and biddeth them that they beware of guile [treachery] in the borough, and standeth together in God's name, and biddeth Piers the Ploughman go to his work and chastise well Hob the Robber and taketh with you John Trueman and all his fellows, and no more, and look schappe you on to heued [i.e. be alert to take heed for your-selves] and no more.

The letter broke into verse:

> John the Miller hath ground small, small, small;
> The King of Heaven's son shall pay for all
> Be ware or be woe,
> Knoweth your friend from your foe,
> Haveth y-now [enough] and say 'Ho' [i.e. 'no more']
> And do well and better, and fleth [i.e. shun] sin,
> And seeketh peace and hold you therein,
> And so biddeth John Trueman and all his fellows.[2]

Clearly, the north was on Ball's mind, as he emphasised both his Yorkshire roots and his Essex links. The covert, almost masonic language of the letters spoke to all his former comrades, and their characterisation as 'John the Miller' and 'John Trueman' was not merely to avoid incriminating potential recipients, but also to conjure up the spirit of the ideal, stout and comradely commons.

Ball, now more than ever, feared treachery and the perversion of the aims of the revolt. The paranoid language in which he counselled his followers to beware of 'guile in the borough' and called for moderation and godly, industrious virtue suggested that as he travelled he saw the original aims of the rebellion slipping from the minds of the splintering movement, subsumed beneath greed and theft.

As he travelled north, he sent more of these letters, using various allegorical pen-names in addition to his own. Sometimes he wrote as 'Jakke Carter', sometimes as 'Jakke Trewman'. In almost all his letters he wrote of a time now arrived, the necessity of holding firm, guarding against deceit and purifying hearts against gluttony, covetousness and plunder.

The letters also indicate a man who felt he still had a claim to the central momentum of the revolt. This, though, was his mistake. For his star, inevitably, was waning. And though he did not know it, as Ball rode up towards the east Midlands that Monday on his way to York, he came within two days' hard ride of another maverick churchman who was about to take charge of the final phase of the topsy-turvy summer.

Henry Despenser, bishop of Norwich, was, like Ball, a man of piety and of action. But he was also a landed aristocrat, a man of the established Church, and a staunch ally of king and Christ. He was a typical member of the lusty class of Edwardian knights: a wealthy young man whose formative years had been spent earning his spurs in battle on the Continent, where, as a vigorous and skilful soldier, he had caught the eye of Pope Urban V. In 1370, when Despenser was just twenty-seven years old, the Pope had seen in him not just the virtues of a soldier, but of a soldier of Christ, and a man who might protect the interests of the Church by his ability to proselytise with his sword as well as his sermons. The normal rules of episcopal appointment had been abrogated in appointing him to the vacant see of Norwich, and for the last eleven years, Despenser had been building a reputation as a bishop with wider concerns than the mere welfare of his flock.

Like Ball, Despenser had seen enough of the revolt in East Anglia to know that Tyler's death and the young king's reported victory at Smithfield were an end as much as a sea-change in the drama of the revolt. Despenser had seen the chaos that was beginning to grip the countryside while he had been travelling at pace across it from Norwich, during the beginning of the weekend, when he had moved from his diocesan throne to the manor of Burleigh in the east Midlands – a family home in a village nestled among forests and the flood plain of the meandering River Gwash.

Despenser's exit from Norwich on Saturday had been well timed, for even as he arrived in Burleigh, the area surrounding the city was falling to a mob under a dyer called Geoffrey Litster. In leaving Norwich, Despenser had avoided a siege at Litster's hands and – potentially – the same fate that had befallen his archbishop in London. Burleigh was a convenient point of safety within two days' hard ride of the seat of his bishopric – a well-armed base on the western edge of the known revolt from where he could safely monitor it without risking capture.

As he had ridden, he had passed north of areas threatened by roaming gangs of insurgents. He managed to avoid any significant encounter with the rebels, but the news reaching him would have promised that very soon he would have to face them.

The countryside would have buzzed with reports of widespread uproar. Property belonging to John of Gaunt was under attack throughout Norfolk, from the coast to the edge of the Fens. Bands of men were riding together throughout the county committing a variety of violent and criminal acts, besieging towns and monasteries and attempting to coerce county gentry to accept leadership of their gangs.

Everywhere he stopped, Despenser would have learned of very serious trouble breaking out around most of the major towns in the east. As well as Litster's rule in and around Norwich, there was uproar in Cambridge, King's Lynn and Ely. Huntingdon was braced for attack as, farther north, was Leicester.

Throughout the region, power had been almost entirely usurped by rebel bands. The most dangerous of these was led by a renegade priest called John Wrawe. Wrawe and his men were peculiarly vicious in their methods, which included extortion, arson, robbery and murder, and were concentrated mainly upon the triangle of land between Cambridge, Bury and Ely.

Wrawe's name must have been known to Despenser by the time he arrived in Burleigh on Sunday, for by that time he and his followers had already smashed and plundered the Priory of St Edmunds at Bury, stolen jewels and treasure worth hundreds of pounds, drunk themselves insensible on wine paid for with plundered goods, blackmailed the town of Thetford and various people of Suffolk for protection payments, ransacked churches, rustled horses and destroyed houses. For those crimes alone Wrawe was already notorious, but in addition to all these things, a band closely sympathetic to his leadership had murdered the Chief Justice of the King's Bench, Sir John Cavendish.

This was a crime as grave as the murders of Sudbury and Hales, and the horror of Cavendish's death by beheading in the village of

Lakenheath on Friday would have rippled out from Bury, where his head was displayed on the pillory in the marketplace. Certainly it would have reached Cambridge, where Cavendish was chancellor of the university, and from there it had no doubt travelled north-west to Burleigh. Terrible stories circulated, recounting games that had been played with the severed heads of Cavendish and John of Cambridge, the prior of Bury St Edmunds: poles had been jammed into their bloodied necks and their heads made to perform grotesque puppet shows, talking together and kissing in imitation of their close relationship in life. The prior's body, stripped to his shirt and breeches, was still lying in an open field, untouched and unburied for fear of the wrath of Wrawe's band.

So by Sunday evening, when he arrived at Burleigh, Bishop Despenser had little time to sit and reflect. In any case, that was not in his nature. Trouble was now virtually at his doorstep. The next day he mustered a small group of armed men – eight lances and a handful of archers – armed himself to the teeth and headed out into the storm.

From Burleigh, Despenser rode east along the course of the river to Stamford. Here news reached him that Peterborough, a few miles south-east, was under attack. The magnificent and modern abbey was one of the richest institutions in England. It housed relics of the murdered martyr St Thomas à Becket and the arm of the Northumbrian king St Oswald. But, more likely, what interested the invaders was the highly visible wealth of the abbey, the head of the abbot and the court rolls and documents relating to large swathes of land, the mills, water tolls and woodlands. Just as at St Albans, there was long-harboured tension between the abbey and its tenants, and chaos provided the perfect environment in which to seek justice.

Relief, however, came not in reasonable protest but in a murderous petty crusade. Despenser arrived to find a wild scene unfolding. The huge, arched west front of the abbey church was besieged; the statues of St Peter, St Paul and St Andrew, high above on the gables, gazed down upon a crowd of neighbours and tenants of the abbey hollering for the abbot's life.[3] They were in a state of high agitation. The country had been further whipped up by news that the renowned knight Sir Robert Salle had been murdered in Norfolk.[4] It was also rumoured that William Ufford, earl of Suffolk, had fled his county disguised as a servant, for fear of capture and subjugation by a rebel band eager to recruit him as a puppet leader of real worship and nobility.

With churchmen and now nobility under siege, it is no surprise that the Peterborough rebels had not anticipated the arrival of a vigorous bishop carrying a large, heavy, double-edged sword. Despenser's men charged the mob, scattering them in terror. Holy compassion was in short supply, and Despenser's small company hacked down all the rebels they could catch.

A number fled into the abbey church, seeking refuge behind the thick Norman walls in the hope of sanctuary under the eyes of God. But the warrior in Despenser prevailed over the churchman. Reasoning that those who had not feared to destroy the ramparts of the church did not deserve its immunity, Despenser pursued the rebels to the altar and his men cut them to ribbons.

There was a certain irony in a bishop rescuing the abbey with a sword, and it did not escape the Lancastrian chronicler Henry Knighton, as he recorded how the confidence of the Peterborough rebels had evaporated once those of their number were either taken prisoner, or slain against the inner and outer walls of the church.

'So was fulfilled the saying of the prophet [i.e. St John the Evangelist],' he wrote, satisfied at the conclusion of this episode. '"You will rule them with iron rods and break them like a potter's vessel."'

For the bishop, however, this was not the fulfilment of his journey, but the beginning. As John Ball, off to the west, stole home towards Yorkshire, Despenser aimed, purposeful and bold, back east to his home in Norwich. Geoffrey Litster, the dyer who hankered to be King of the Commons, was preparing to enter the city, forcing knights to act as his servants and extorting protection money from the towns-folk. The king and council were barely reasserting their grip on power around London – there would be no help from the government for the foreseeable future. To all practical ends, the security of the whole of East Anglia now fell under the protection of Despenser. The bishop secured his prisoners and turned his sights south, towards Huntingdon.

TWENTY

COUNTER-TERROR

John Balle seynte Marye prist gretes wele alle maner men and byddes
hem in the name of the Trinite, Fadur, and Sone and Holy Gost stoned
manlyche togedyr in trewthe, and helpez trewthe, and trewthe schal
helpe yowe. Now regnith pride in pris and covetys is hold wys, and
leccherye withouten shame and glotonye withouten blame. Envye
regnith with treson and slouthe is take in grete sesone. God do bote,
for nowe is tyme amen.

Letter from John Ball, preserved by Henry Knighton

Tuesday, 18 June–Wednesday, 19 June
Two full days had passed since London had been emptied of rebels,
and at last Richard and his council could begin to establish some
sense of structure to government.

In London, the proceedings of the extraordinary commission
awarded to Walworth and the aldermen became active. With the
powers of mutilation, decapitation and summary, extralegal justice,
reprisals were swift and brutal. 'Gibbets arose where none had been
before, since existing ones were too few for the bodies of the
condemned,' remembered the Westminster chronicler.

In the busy thoroughfare at Cheap, where the blood that had
spilled out of the rebels' victims was barely washed away, a new block
was erected. Speed was of the essence in executing anyone condemned
for taking part in the rising. Some of the guilty were beheaded, others

hanged before decapitation. Royal law was now responsible for the gore that congealed in the straw and dirt of the streets, and it would have been a shocking scene even to a City so recently privy to the same acts at the hands of the rebels. Royal law was usually expected to act with restraint in equal measure to the awful symbolism of ritual public punishment.

But Walworth's justice was chillingly biblical. It was less a case of an eye for an eye, and more a head for a head. Flemings from the riverside communities massacred by the rebels were allowed to execute with their own hands the rebels found guilty of taking part in the slayings. Flemish wives struggled with heavy axes and killed their husbands' murderers. London's executioners were no impartial agents of justice, but friends to murdered men, and axe-wielding widows.[1]

If the punishments were severe it was because to Richard and the council, clemency after the ordeal could not be countenanced. Following his show of royal magnanimity at Smithfield, the young king had hardened his heart. No longer fearful for his life and the City's immediate safety, panic turned to anger. An English king slighted was a dangerous prospect, and early in life Richard began to display the same easily fanned tendency towards vengeance that Plantagenet kings right back to Henry II had demonstrated.

Having provided for the security of London, on Tuesday, 18 June, he witnessed by his own hand a commission that went out 'to each and every one of the sheriffs, mayors, bailiffs and others of our loyal subjects' in the shires, calling them to oppose by force all rebels against the peace. Far from being a dry legal formality, Richard's commission fairly bristled with rage: 'We would have you know through this present letter that it is not at all with our approval or authority that [various rebellious subjects] have gone ahead with such risings, assemblies, and harmful deeds, for these should not have been planned or carried out,' he wrote, tartly.

'Indeed,' the commission continued, 'our displeasure resulting from these deeds could not be greater than it is, and we feel that their actions have been a very great insult to us, injurious to the crown, and harmful and disturbing to the whole of our kingdom.'[2]

These letters sped across the country, arriving within days in the English shires that remained turbulent and hot with conspiracy and confederations. All the country now knew the king was wrathful.

In East Anglia, however, news of the king's wrath was barely beginning to affect the enthusiasm of the rebel bands that pocketed the shires. The bloody murders committed under John Wrawe at Bury St Edmunds ended with the news from London that Tyler had been vanquished, but north of Suffolk the mayhem continued. Manors across Norfolk and Cambridgeshire continued to be plagued by rioting crowds demanding their ancient liberties and burning court rolls and other symbols of land tenure and lordship. Unlike in London, there was scant thought for reforming the realm at large; by and large it was individual disputes which were pursued.

The widespread violence put an extreme skittishness into the hearts of lords and local governors across England. Henry Knighton recalled how 'the hearts of all men in every part of the realm, however remote, trembled with fear of the rebels; and everywhere it was fearfully believed that the rebels were about to arrive in person and without warning'. In Leicester itself the mayor had everyone in the town arm themselves in preparation for the arrival of a rebel band rumoured to be marching from Harborough, about five miles to the south-east. The band never came, but the fear was such that the abbot refused to store in Leicester Abbey any valuable property belonging to the duke of Lancaster. Gaunt was a marked man in one of his own towns: his possessions had already been cleared out of the town's castle in the hope of avoiding a repeat of the nightmare at the Savoy.

In tandem with the rising paranoia across the country, there was a disturbing development to the rebellion in Norfolk. Several local gentry were rumoured to have assumed leadership of bands of rebels. Geoffrey Litster was backed in Norwich by Sir Roger Bacon, who had helped lead the storming of the city, riding at the head of the rebel band, decked out as if for war, flags fluttering above him. This was a serious development, showing as it did that the social boundaries of rebellion were expanding dangerously.

Amid all this, however, there was one important pocket of East Anglian authority. At the centre was Despenser. Following his success at Peterborough, Despenser and his well-armed retinue started to gather in their orbit the first coherent armed band of loyalists in the region. By Tuesday 18th the effect was beginning to be seen on the triangular region of fenland between Peterborough, Huntingdon and Ely.

Late the previous evening a party of commons had passed by the small town of Huntingdon, on their way north, where – according to one chronicler – 'in their malice and villainy they intended to ravage the land and destroy good men'.[3] Huntingdon was a necessary stage on the route north that linked London, Lincoln and York, because its large, five-arched stone bridge over the River Ouse, which had been erected in the 1330s, was the principal crossing point in the region.

It was most likely a combination of the added geographical security that the river border offered, the cheering news of Despenser's progress through the Fens and a steeliness of collective nerve which emboldened Huntingdon's townsmen. When the rebels arrived at the bridge, they encountered a belligerent crowd. William Wightman, an official from the Westminster bureaucracy, headed the townsmen, who must have been well armed, for they gave battle to the rebels, killing two or three and putting the rest to flight. It was a small but important victory, later rewarded by the king, who in December publicly thanked the borough for its loyalty and who the next year awarded Wightman a pension for his actions in repelling the invaders. They were deserved accolades: the little town of Huntingdon had shown greater spirit in defending its bridge than all London had shown on Corpus Christi.

That spirit travelled on the air a couple of miles north to Ramsey Abbey, where a band of rebels from Ely had been blackmailing the abbot in much the same manner as was occurring all across East Anglia – where the standard form was to invoke the menacing prospect of either John Wrawe or the late Wat Tyler sending thousands of rampaging commons unless liberties and court rolls were handed over. The Ely rebels had spent much of the night camped in Ramsey town, dining and drinking themselves to satiety on bread, wine, ale and other supplies they had extorted from the abbey. Consequently, they had been late rising that morning.

Hung over – or, at the very least, tired and confused – they presented an easy target for Despenser. His retinue bolstered by the men of Huntingdon keen to follow up their earlier victory, he laid into the rebel band, in what seems to have been an uneven skirmish. Those that fled were chased down and dispatched by the roadside. The trees around the towns, villages and highways of Huntingdonshire were decorated with the severed heads of the insurgents as a warning to anyone considering an attack on this remarkably resilient outpost of order.

And so Despenser pushed on towards his diocese. So far he had seen little to test his zeal. But the road back to Norwich was still littered with danger. From Huntingdon the bishop turned east, and set out towards Cambridge.

He reached the small university town on 19 June, arriving from the north-west. The castle that sat on the lone hill that emerged from the surrounding fenlands cast an impotent shadow over the troubled settlement below it. Travelling the relatively short distance from Huntingdon, Despenser would have heard of severe unrest in Cambridge.[4] It had been caused by a combination of townsmen and agitators from the county. Rioting began with attacks on property belonging to a local landowner and Crown agent, Roger of Harleston, and spread outwards, involving factions from the whole of Cambridge society.

Harleston was one of the principal victims – he had been roundly punished for his inflammatory status in both town and county community. He was a burgess of the town and a conspicuously wealthy one, at that. But he was also tightly connected to the county administration, having held office as an MP, and a commissioner both for the labour laws and the poll tax. He was an aggressively acquisitive office-holder and land speculator with recent and lavish wealth throughout the town and the outlying county manors. In his unfortunate person was summed up every iniquity resented by the rebels at large, and his property paid the price in the days of rioting that took place over Corpus Christi weekend.

But as Despenser rode into town, he saw more than simply the piecemeal destruction of one wealthy social climber's property portfolio. The town was a mess. Its economic and religious centres had been roundly despoiled. St Mary's church, which had been terrorised and plundered on Sunday, bore the scars of a rambunctious desecration. Jewels and plate had been stolen, and the great university chest, in which were kept important documents and muniments pertaining to the scholars' administration of their considerable jurisdiction in Cambridge, had been forcibly opened and raided.

Riding a hundred yards or so along the road, Despenser would have seen Corpus Christi College, which had also been invaded, and its books, letters, charters and other documents taken from it. The Carmelite house had suffered the same fate. Elsewhere a house belonging to the university bedel, William Wigmore, had been looted and destroyed.

The marketplace bore the signs of another riot. On Sunday, Despenser would have discovered, with merely the slightest of effort, that a great bonfire had been held to consign to oblivion all those charters that had been gathered from university strongrooms. A mob had gathered about the flames to throw in the plundered parchment. Ash mingled on the ground with thin slivers of sealing wax, scratched away from documents with sticks, knives and whatever other weapons had come to hand. A townswoman by the name of Marjery Starr had achieved brief notoriety for throwing ash up to blow about in the summer air, while shouting 'Away with the learning of the clerks! Away with it!'

Marjery Starr's spirit of jubilant vandalism had stolen into the whole city, and a mob comprising both townsmen and country rebels had laid waste the parks and property belonging to Barnwell Priory, a little way out from the town centre. The prior had been terrorised into signing a bond worth £2000 to submit to the rebels' will. With

John Cavendish, chancellor of the university, several days dead at the hands of Wrawe sympathisers, there was little choice for the university members but to follow suit; they had £3000 extorted from them, as well as a series of agreements concerning civil governance that were skewed as heavily in the townsmen's favour as those previous had been against them.

Like the town, the surrounding countryside had also suffered. The roads in and out of town had been trampled in both directions by hoofs and human feet alike. County men, some of whom had been at least inspired by, and possibly even in contact with, Tyler's rebels, had come to town to join in the attacks on Harleston's townhouses; returning the favour, men from the town – including the first movers in the anti-Harleston riots at Cottenham on 9 June – had gone frequently in the opposite direction. As many as 160 mounted townsmen had ridden out on Saturday to the hospital at Shingay and the two manors at Steeple Morden and Giles (Guilden) Morden to join attacks inspired by county men who resented both the Hospitallers and the local landowner, Thomas Hasilden.

It is a shame that no record of Despenser's conversation with Mayor Edmund Lister of Cambridge exists, for the bishop would have surely had some coruscating words for the supposed civic leader concerning his role in the city riots. Unlike in London and the other major towns affected by the revolt, the town hierarchy was extremely prominent in leading the rebellion. The mayor, claiming he had acted under duress and in the belief that the king had sided with the insurgents, had led them throughout much of the weekend, most notably against the university and the Priory of Barnwell. It was – Despenser would have seen – fairly clear that the county element of the Cambridge mob had been emboldened and enfranchised by the leadership, whether enthusiastic or otherwise, of mayor and burgesses.

Whatever was said by Despenser to Lister, it seems to have been effective, because, unlike in Peterborough and Huntingdonshire, there appears to have been little need for the bishop to show off his military competence. News of his own approach and the king's extreme displeasure with rebels throughout his realm had arrived the previous day, swiftly winding down the rebellion. The town and countryside had been turned upside down, but there had been relatively little bloodshed, and no display of armed resistance. The matters of damaged property and extorted charters were serious, but could not merit summary justice against the upper reaches of the town's hierarchy for fear of reducing the town to total anarchy. There was already quite enough of that in the surrounding countryside.

And with Cambridge, Despenser was closing in on his diocese. To get there he had to pass through one of the most dangerous and lawless parts of the country. What was left of Norwich, and who now ruled, he could not have known for sure. There was only one way to find out.

TWENTY-ONE

NORWICH

The bishop hurried towards Norwich, moving to North Walsham, the place the commons had chosen to wait for the King's reply and the return of their colleagues. As the bishop crossed through the country the number of his forces increased. The knights and gentlemen of the area who had previously lain low for fear of the commons joined the bishop's side when they saw him dressed as a knight, wearing an iron helm and a solid hauberk impregnable to arrows as he wielded a real two-edged sword . . .

THOMAS WALSINGHAM

East Anglia, Saturday, 22 June

Moving north-east towards his diocesan seat in Norwich, every mile took Despenser closer to the most perilous area of the revolt. Its western fringes, in which he had dismissed and dispatched bands of urban and rural rebels with a dashing combination of military aggression and ecclesiastical pomp, were its least organised. But as he pushed in the direction of the Norfolk coast, Despenser was riding into the rebel heartlands.

Norfolk, as the most northerly county to experience truly widespread rioting, was also the latest to rise. Whereas Suffolk and Cambridgeshire had both been infected with rebellion from Essex since before Corpus Christi, the eastern parts of Norfolk had remained calm until Monday 17th, when Despenser was far away at Burleigh.

Since then, nine of the fourteen peace commissioners for Norfolk, who had been appointed in November and December 1380, had been marked for attacks by the county commons. They included John of Gaunt, who owned property in the north-east of the county, William Ufford, duke of Suffolk, Robert Howard, Stephen Hales, Reginald de Ecceles and others.[1] The bishop's own manor at Hevingham had been plundered and its records burned.

During the previous weekend, rebel agitators had ridden through the villages of north-east Norfolk, inciting the local people to insurrection. And on that Monday, villagers from across the county had beaten a steady path towards Mousehold Heath, a large, rolling patch of heathland and forest close to Norwich.

They had gathered under the leadership of Litster, a dyer from the village of Felmingham. Litster seems, like Tyler and Ball, to have been capable of commanding large ranks of men by the force of his natural charisma, and he had associates responsible for some isolated rioting in the west of the county. He was also able to bring to his movement a calibre of support that made it very dangerous indeed: the presence of a significant number of Norfolk gentlemen.

Chief among Litster's associates was Sir Roger Bacon. Bacon was a knight of Baconsthorpe, a manor some six miles from the north Norfolk coast, and half a day's hard ride from Norwich. The cause of Bacon's disgruntlement with the politics of the region and nation is obscure, but he very clearly held the nascent hierarchy in poor enough regard to risk his position by throwing in his lot with the rebel movement, knowing as he did so that he added immeasurably to the strength of the Norfolk insurgents.

Along with Bacon, Litster could count on the support of several other well-to-do county dignitaries, including Thomas Gyssing, son of one Sir Thomas Gyssing, who had sat as an MP for Norfolk in 1380. And the rebels were numerous enough and sufficiently threatening also to coerce others of the gentry into joining them. Sir Roger Scales, Sir Thomas Morley, Sir John de Brewes and Sir Stephen Hales, a poll tax controller, were all captured and forced to serve with Litster.

In mixing with gentry, Litster seems to have been indulging a fantasy of regality. As soon as his leadership was established, he began to style himself as 'King of the Commons' – a position that reflected a common medieval type played out in the deliberately topsy-turvy summer games that were played at village festivals. Litster, however, set out permanently to invert the tradition. He forced Scales, Morley, Brewes and Hales to do his bidding as courtly servants, tasting his food and attending to a variety of similarly menial tasks. Litster doubtless took as much pleasure in the ritual humiliation of his social betters as he did in indulging his lofty social ambition – he may also have been dabbling with the ideology of restoring the kingdoms of the commons.

Whatever it was that motivated him, he had, on that Monday, assembled a large and willing crowd on Mousehold Heath. The target was Norwich. When the respected courtly knight and war veteran Sir Robert Salle rode out from the city to attempt negotiations, he was dragged from his horse and murdered.[2] It was a taste of what was to follow.

In Norwich, Tuesday, 18 June was remembered as a day of bloodshed and plunder. Litster's huge band swarmed in from the heath, entered the city – led by Bacon – and embarked upon a vicious orgy of violence and rapine. Huge crowds tore into the houses of those connected with the law and with royal government (one prosecution after the revolt named 800 defendants for a single attack). Salle's house was smashed and robbed. The wealthy citizen Henry Lominor, who, like Salle, had been an MP in 1378, was robbed of goods worth 1000 marks. Reginald Eccles, a Justice of the Peace, had been snatched by a mob from his manor lodgings in Heigham; his house was looted, rebels making off with goods including his furred official gown. He was brought into the city melee, dragged to the pillory, stabbed in the stomach and beheaded.

Tax collectors were, naturally, at great peril, and Walter de Bixton, who represented the city at the parliaments where poll taxes had been granted, and was subsequently appointed a collector, had his house broken into and pillaged. John de Freston, archdeacon of Norwich, suffered similarly. The only way that marked townspeople could seek protection was by paying extortionate ransoms to protect their property.

As Norwich suffered, outbreaks of violence erupted right across the county. On the 18th, while Despenser was in Peterborough, there were riots in Rougham and Wyghton, Langford and Southery. One Robert de Gravele narrowly escaped death, agreeing, as his head was held on the block, to pay his tormenters 8 marks, 16 pence and 28 cows in return for his life.

By the next morning, the 19th, while Despenser was in Cambridge, the Norwich rebels had splintered outwards. They behaved more like the Essex men than the Kentishmen, dispersing around the county in small groups to pursue private quarrels, and indulge themselves in largely aimless plunder and extortion. Bacon and Litster headed east, taking a band across the broads and the marshland that sprawled out along the banks of the River Yare and on towards the coast to Great Yarmouth. There was a long-standing dispute at Yarmouth concerning the jurisdiction of a nearby port, and rights to the herring trade on which the town was built.

On arriving at Yarmouth the rebels broke open the jail and freed all the prisoners but three Flemings, whom they beheaded. Rioting ensued, and the houses of local gentlemen were smashed. The town's charter of liberties was extracted from the town's burgesses by menace; Bacon and Litster had it torn in two, and sent one half the few miles down the coast and across the county border into Suffolk, where they understood Wrawe was fomenting trouble around Beccles and Lowestoft. Bacon then turned north, riding along the coast and up to Winterton, stopping on the way to plunder and extort ransoms in Caister. Litster, too, went north, heading towards North Walsham and Thorpe Market.

Having destroyed their county town, and surely realising that the wrath of the Crown would not be delayed indefinitely, by the end of the week Bacon and Litster had run out of steam. Their followers were scattered about the county, and Wrawe had retreated from Beccles back towards Essex. Bacon seems to have tired of action, and brought his part in the rampage to an end.

Litster, however, had warmed to the grandeur, and by Friday, 21 June, he was to be found at Thorpe Market, comporting himself in as grand a fashion as befitted the King of the Commons. There were attacks on John of Gaunt's manors around Gimingham, and extensive burning of court rolls. There were outbursts in Mundesley, Knapton, Southrepps, Northrepps, Sidestrand, Trunch and other places. There were similar extensive attacks on the manors of the abbey of St Benets-at-Holme in the Flegg. Litster's men still rode about the countryside proclaiming the rising in his name.

Yet for all these noisome efforts, Litster's revolt was splintering and beginning to lack structure or direction. Accordingly, at the end of the week, as Despenser was leaving Cambridge, Litster had decided to seek a resolution to his game. He sent two of his knightly retinue, Sir Thomas Morley and Sir John de Brewes, along with three of his trusted commons – John Trunch of Trunch, William Kybyte of Worstead and Thomas Skeet also of Worstead – with instructions to seek out the king and lobby for a pardon and a grant of manumission. As leverage for this royal charter, they provided the party with a large sum of money extorted earlier in the week from the citizens of Norwich as an alternative to having their houses fired and their lives extinguished.

Laden down with plundered wealth and heavy expectations, Litster's envoys took the road south-west out of Norwich. Unfortunately for the commons in the party, they were passing along the very same road as, and in the direction of, Bishop Despenser. Close to the village of Icklingham, in south-west Norfolk, on the edge of the king's forest, at a spot where a watermill narrowed the road, the two parties met.

Having sent one of their number away to find victuals, the rebel party was one man down when they met the bishop. Nevertheless, the ragtag quartet he encountered struck Despenser as odd. As they approached, he greeted the knights, and ordered them to declare on their loyalty whether there were any traitors to the king present in their party.

This presented Morley and Brewes with a dilemma. Their service as Litster's knights attendant had been uncomfortable and distressing. Even as they had been granted leave to find Richard II, Brewes' manor at Heydon had been robbed by the rebels and his manorial court records burned. The sight of the professionally armed and well-supported bishop would have been a welcome glimpse of a return to order. On the other hand, their treatment under the commons had turned their world so firmly upside down that they had all but lost hope of rescue. Numbers were now strongly in their favour, but who knew what the reaction of the commons at large might be if they were ever discovered to have betrayed their captors? Frightened and uncertain, they told Despenser that everything was well.

Despenser saw straight through their fiction. He asked them a second time, pleading with them to have confidence in him and deliver up any traitors who were with them. His iron will was effective, and the knights took courage. They told Despenser that they had two of the greatest leaders of sedition in the county with them, while a third was foraging somewhere for their next meal. They told the bishop everything that had happened to them, and the purpose of their mission out of the county.

The bishop understood it all.

A little farther along the road was the small town of Newmarket. When Bishop Despenser's party arrived there, they nailed up for public view the three freshly severed heads of Skeet, Trunch and Kybyte.[3]

Back in London, Richard and his court now felt secure enough to leave the City. The military commission under Walworth had restored public order, and re-established the disrupted flow of victuals into London, backed as he was by the power to use armed escorts to protect suppliers passing through the simmering countryside.

To ensure the loyalty of the citizens, on Thursday 20th Walworth had commanded the aldermen to take an oath of fealty from everyone in their wards, and to arrest anyone who refused. And the judicial commission to punish rebels, over which Walworth and Chief Justice Robert Belknap presided, had been meeting in the Guildhall all week. It was preparing to deliver by the following Monday all those prisoners that had been taken and were now held in Newgate jail.

With London restored to capable hands, Richard could contemplate turning his attention to the rest of the country. He still sorely missed the presence of Gaunt, whose personal influence over vast stretches of England through the duchy of Lancaster would have been immensely valuable in bringing the realm to order. But Gaunt had problems of his own, way in the north of the country. Despite having known privately of the disaster that had befallen the country and his own palace of the Savoy on Corpus Christi, the duke had held his nerve during the talks and negotiated a favourable peace treaty with the Scots from a position of extraordinary weakness. He left the chilly east coast border town of Coldingham, near Berwick, on the 20th to attempt to bring his retinue south to help his nephew.

Unfortunately, ill news had blown hard north. Wild rumours and distortions of what had passed at Mile End had consumed the country. It was said that the government had heard that Gaunt was bringing an army of 20,000 to seize the Crown for himself, and had accordingly declared him a traitor. Muddying this was the rumour that he had freed all the serfs on his estates, and was preparing to sweep into power at the head of a peasant army.

Of course, none of this was true, but Gaunt had enemies enough who were willing to believe the worst. These included the earl of Northumberland, Henry Percy. Percy sent Gaunt a message stating that he could offer him no reception or hospitality without the king's explicit approval. The promise was made good when the duke reached the castle of Bamburgh to find its gates locked, on the earl's command. Gaunt was forced to return north and throw himself on the hospitality of the Scots. Some four hundred miles from the worst crisis of order the country had ever known, the most experienced and powerful noble in the land was left exiled and impotent.

Events outran the speed of communication between the king and his uncle, so it was not for another week that Richard could send orders for Gaunt's honourable protection in returning to England. In the meantime, he could take solace in the return of the earl of Buckingham, who was supported by an army from Brittany that had been intended for the harassment of the French.

Accordingly, on Thursday, 20 June, while Despenser was preparing to enter Norfolk and Walworth was taking oaths of good behaviour in London, Richard began to issue commissions to fight, try and punish rebels across the country.

The first commission went to Robert Tresilian, a senior judge who was now invested as Chief Justice of the Court of King's Bench to replace the murdered Cavendish. Tresilian was a tough, unscrupulous Cornishman, who was both legally astute and personally intimidating. He was the perfect candidate to accompany Richard in person, a hanging judge to travel with the court out of London and into the shires. The second commission went to Buckingham, who was empowered to take his large armed force wherever it was required across the country to quell the revolt, but directed in the first instance towards the birthplace of the troubles: Essex. This commission required less in the way of legal finesse; rather, it was a blunt military instrument intended to hammer the rebels into submission.

With these first commissions established, the court moved. On Saturday, the king headed for Waltham, an abbey town in the southwest corner of Essex, right on the border with Hertfordshire. To get there, he would have taken the Bishopsgate out of the trembling City. The road that took him north led past the smoking husk of Hales' manor in Highbury. This ugly reminder of the damage that had been done to the realm would have heaped fuel on to the young king's furious heart.

When he arrived in Waltham, he prepared further punitive commissions. He sent his half-brother Thomas Holland into his new earldom of Kent to vanquish the rump of the rebellion there. William Ufford, earl of Suffolk, who had been forced to flee from John Wrawe's rebels, was sent back into East Anglia with 500 lances to follow Despenser's vanguard and pacify Norfolk and Suffolk. Suffolk headed first for Bury, where the most heinous crimes had taken place.

The tide, now, was turning. And so was Richard. Finally backed by military and judicial force, he prepared to take his full revenge on the rebels. He was no longer the benevolent boy who had captained his commons at Smithfield, and let them slip back home unharmed.

Now emerged a side of his personality that England would come to experience with terrible relentlessness during the course of his reign: cruel, obsessive vengeance.

TWENTY-TWO

VENGEANCE

The populace shuddered at the spectacle of so many gibbeted bodies exposed to the light of day . . . Despite all the retribution thus visited on the guilty the severity of the royal displeasure seemed to be in no way mitigated but rather to be directed with increased harshness towards the punishment of offenders . . . It was widely thought that in the circumstances the king's generous nature ought to exercise leniency rather than vindictiveness . . .

Westminster Chronicle

The firmer the grip Richard and his officers retook of the realm, the tougher they seemed to want to be. Lenience was not forthcoming.

At the end of June, this was understandable. The rebellious spirit was infectious. Even as Richard moved out of the City and into Essex, there was trouble from the West Country to the northern marches.

In Bridgwater, Somerset, the townspeople, in collusion with various willing accomplices drawn from the local gentry, had during the past week indulged in a typically gluttonous programme of violence. They had begun by bullying the inhabitants of the Augustinian Hospital of St John, and progressed to extortion, theft, charter-burning, jail-breaking and murder.

Likewise, in York, the spirit of violence had turned long-running and complex political grievances between factions among the citizens into open internal warfare. Again, attacks had been made on local religious houses, and serious trouble was fomenting by the end of June between factions attached to rivals for the office of mayor.

In character, if not method, isolated spates of urban uproar bore little relation to anything which Wat Tyler or John Ball had originally envisaged when they had been marching on London. They contained nothing but political point-scoring and violent rapacity. But they were problematic, as they both sprang from and furthered the countrywide spirit of chaos and disorder. That spirit had somehow to be quashed, and Richard's methods were severe.

He split the rebellious parts of England into neat packages. Having sent commissions to the most troubled counties, Richard empowered them with extraordinary military and judicial discretion. Due process of law was to be applied in trying the rebels where practical, but the commissioners were authorised to keep or restore order or to settle cases by any other means they saw fit. The highways of England would have rumbled to the sound of these heavily armed commissions coming to bring military justice to the people. Judgement was always supposed to be awe-inspiring, but now it would have been terrifying. It was merciless and unrestrained, and it was brought in warlike fashion, rather than with wisdom and responsibility.[1]

The earl of Buckingham had been sent with his considerable army to pacify Essex. That Richard deployed his weightiest military resources in that direction was testimony to the volatile nature of the county. Though there had been Essex men in London and at Mile End, many of the first movers of rebellion had concentrated on terrorising their own county. There had been severe rioting, particularly along the east coast and in the stretch of countryside between Chelmsford and Colchester. There was still dangerous tension around the former, where the greatest public burning of county records had taken place on 11 June, and Buckingham wasted little time in opening sessions there.

But Essex was barely ready for peace sessions. Revolutionary fervour remained. And so, as Buckingham's commission sat on Tuesday 25th, it was approached by one John Preston, a resident of Hadleigh, a small town west of Ipswich, not far inside the Suffolk border. Preston had presumably been active in one of the bands that played havoc across the Suffolk and Essex border. He was certainly one of the more ideologically literate rebels, but possibly one of the more politically naive, for he brought before Buckingham a written petition of demands, intended for the king.

Preston's petition addressed Richard on behalf of the commons, and rehearsed again the demands for manumission of serfs and a fixed rent of 4d an acre made at Mile End. In effect, it was a request for confirmation of the charters that had been extorted from the Crown under the traumatic invasion of London.

Buckingham's commission must have looked on Preston with disbelief. They had him immediately arrested and brought before them for questioning. The commissioners asked him who had produced the petition. He admitted that it was his work. Incredulous, they asked him who had delivered it to them, and again – there was little point in denying it – Preston said that he had brought it. He was immediately beheaded.[2]

If this seemed like rough justice for behaviour that at any other time would barely have been seditious, let alone treasonable, it was a mark both of the nervousness and of the arbitrary power of Richard's commissions.

Such were the times. Ascribing such wide-ranging powers to his commissioners served to embolden the English nobility to act with the decisiveness and purpose shown by Bishop Despenser on his grand foray across East Anglia. And it was under Despenser that the next decisive event of the week took place. The bishop had finally reached Norwich on the weekend, at the same time as Richard was settling at Waltham. Despenser was, even in late June, still acting unsanctioned by the royal government, but he was playing a vital role in arresting any further development of rebellion. Commissioners rode hard behind him, to secure what he had won – Hugh de la Zouche in Cambridgeshire was seeking to track down and execute the Cambridgeshire rebel leader John Hauchach, while the earl of Suffolk was dispatched to begin restoring the East Anglian peace in his own county – but Despenser himself had one last target. It was one of honour as much of necessity, and it was also one of great symbolism. His target was the head of Geoffrey Litster.

Sensing his quarry near, Despenser had ridden into Norwich on Monday, 24 June, attended by an array of Norfolk's knights and gentlemen, drawn to his side as he travelled through the countryside. The party entered Norwich to find the city despoiled, but no sign of his man. The King of the Commons was away in the countryside, holding court around the North Walsham area. After a short delay to help pacify the city, by Wednesday 26th Despenser was ready. He organised his company and set out from the city for his long-awaited confrontation with the architect of Norwich's destruction.

Litster was waiting. On hearing that the bishop had arrived in Norwich, he sent riders thundering through the villages of north Norfolk, holding assemblies against the bishop, recruiting men and attempting to restore the unity that was last seen on Mousehold Heath. After two days of frantic conscription, they managed to recruit a semblance of an army, based just south of North Walsham.

The rebel army dug in. There was but rudimentary field experience among the ranks, and they arranged themselves as best they could to await Despenser's arrival. A military ditch was fashioned around the place of assembly, and it was reinforced with tables, shutters and gates, all held together with wooden stakes. They barricaded the rear with carts and carriages.[3]

Whatever slight military know-how lay behind the rebel fortifications, it was no match for the bishop's knightly training. Years spent close to the action in the French wars had hardened him to tough enemies and unfavourable odds. A peasant army underwritten by a few hasty earthworks and a higgledy-piggledy wagon train was hardly intimidating.

He led his small armed band towards the rebels, and with a command fired by all his righteous indignation, called his buglers and trumpeters to sound, seized a lance and charged. His display of leadership and military skill left a lasting impression on his contemporaries – Thomas Walsingham likened him to 'a wild boar gnashing its teeth' – and he scattered the rebel ranks in a whirlwind of vicious hand-to-hand combat.

Very rapidly the carts that made up the rebels' rear defences became more attractive as getaway vehicles, and there was a rush among Litster's men to mount them and flee. But, as in Huntingdon, Despenser gave orders to hunt down the deserters, who were struck down until the bishop had vanquished the whole sorry rebel rearguard.

Finally, amid the melee, Litster was captured, and the fighting drew to an end. Despenser used the discretionary powers he had assumed to himself as the diocesan avenging angel and sentenced the King of the Commons to a traitor's death.

Yet for all his furious heroics, Despenser did not forget that he had a pastoral duty, even to the most errant of his flock. He confessed and absolved Litster as his office demanded, and as the condemned man was dragged to the gallows, Despenser held up his head to prevent it from banging on the ground.

It was a small mercy; Litster was hanged, then cut down and his bowels cut from his body and burned in front of him, before finally being beheaded. His body was cut into four pieces. Three were sent to Yarmouth, Norwich and Lynn. The last was nailed up outside his house in Framlingham, as a reminder to all who passed by what happened to false kings.

Richard, still at Waltham, would have heard of all of this with satisfaction. His honour was being restored, and the memory of the shame brought upon his royal dignity was being erased. But there was work still to do, and the audacity of the commons continued to surprise the court.

Driven back from Chelmsford by Buckingham's presence, crowds of Essex rebels had begun to gather a few miles to the south, around the village of Rettenden, near Billericay. 'Trusting too much in their own strength,' wrote one observer, 'and deceived by their own pride they determined either to enjoy the liberty they sought by violence or to die in fighting for it.'[4]

Probably at the same time that Richard Preston was sent to treat for the rebels' liberties with Buckingham, envoys were sent east to Waltham, to plead the same case before the king and council. They asked once again for their liberty to be equal with that of the lords, and for freedom from enforced appearance before the courts.

The request, as at Chelmsford, met only with astonishment at the rebels' temerity. For a time, Richard and his council deliberated on the best course of action. There was, as with Buckingham, a reasonable precedent for instant retribution; but Richard was either minded or persuaded to respect the traditional rights of envoys.

Rather than beheading them, he delivered to them a personal speech that could have left the commons in no doubt whatever that the pact between 'King Richard and the trew commons' was exposed as utterly false. Walsingham recorded the king's words, and even if there was a poetic licence to his rendition, the sentiment was undoubtedly preserved:

> Oh! You wretches, hateful on land and sea, and not worthy to live, who demand to be made equal to your lords. You would certainly have died a most ignominious death if we had not determined to observe the rights of envoys . . .
>
> Give this message to your colleagues from the King. Villeins you are, and villeins you will remain; in permanent bondage, not as it was before, but incomparably harsher . . .
>
> While by God's grace we rule over this kingdom, we shall strive . . . to keep you in subjection, to such a degree that the suffering of your servitude may serve as an example to posterity, and that now and in the future men like you may ever have before your eyes your present misery as something to contemplate, a reason for cursing you and for fearing to perpetrate crimes like yours.[5]

The rebels departed, the young king's scolding hanging dark in the air behind them, and the rumble of an avenging army hard on their heels. Two days later, on Friday, 28 June, exactly two weeks after the Kent, Essex and London rebels had besieged the Tower of London, taunted their king and the great burgesses of London on their way to Mile End, dragged Flemings from sanctuary and flooded the streets of the capital with blood, the stage was finally set for royal retribution.

The court had crossed Hainault Forest to Havering-atte-Bower, five miles east of the rebel camp in Billericay. Between them was Brentwood, where Thomas Baker's assaults on the poll tax commissioners had lit the first flames of revolt. Like Litster's men, the Essex rebels had dug in, hundreds of men fortifying the woodland's natural defences with ditches, stakes and carts.

Like Litster's rebels, their rudimentary defences were hopeless. Buckingham and Lord Thomas Percy marched on Billericay and sent a small company of ten lances into the woods to drive out their target.

With heavily armed soldiers piling through the undergrowth, the stand descended swifly into chaos. The rebel positions were scattered, hopeless against heavy cavalry, and the forest erupted with frightened men fleeing for their lives. All they found as they broke cover, though, was the main body of Buckingham's encircling army. Those who survived abandoned their horses and possessions and hiked north to Colchester, and then to the Suffolk border and Sudbury – no doubt hoping vainly to find John Wrawe still active there. But John Wrawe was gone, and behind them, relentless and well supported, came Buckingham's knights Sir William Fitzwalter and Sir John Harleston, full ready to pick off the weak, and imprison the lucky ones.

The rest of the Essex rebels – perhaps five hundred of them in all – eventually ran confused and indisciplined from the Billericay woods, the place where everything had begun, and exposed themselves, ramshackle and totally vulnerable. They were cut down without mercy as they poured out from among the trees.

EPILOGUE

Ye came as helpless infants to the world:
Ye feel alike the infirmities of nature;
And at last moulder into common clay.

From 'Wat Tyler' by Robert Southey

John Ball was captured by the men of Coventry during his escape north. The exact date is not recorded, but it was most likely in the second week of July, following about three and a half weeks on the road. He was sent for trial to St Albans, which the king had made his base while London suffered a summer plague that preyed, in particular, on the children.

Ball's crimes and wicked deeds were rehearsed in detail at his trial before the remorseless Sir Robert Tresilian. The men of St Albans heard how Ball had corrupted the English people for more than twenty years, preaching perfidious doctrines about the Church and the lords both from the pulpit and in the country fields. He was accused of being a Wycliffite and an incorrigible excommunicant who had roused the rabble at Blackheath and incited Sudbury's death. One of the many cryptic letters that had been circulating the country was produced – this one was addressed to the Essex commons – and Ball admitted to having written it. After Ball was sentenced, the bishop of London, William Courtenay, interceded and secured him a few days' stay of execution, to try to persuade him to repent. There is no record of his having done so. Ball was hanged, beheaded, disembowelled and quartered, and his butchered body was sent to four parts of the country. He died on Monday, 15 July 1381, exactly one month after Smithfield.

Ball's death was the biggest coup in Richard and Tresilian's campaign to extinguish the last flickers of rebellion. But huge numbers of trials and executions followed, and by mid-July, John Wrawe, William Grindcobbe, Jack Straw and almost every other significant rebel leader was also captured or dead. (At the same time as Ball was being tried in St Albans, Wrawe turned approver, or king's evidence, before the sheriffs and coroners of London.) On the day following Ball's death the realm was deemed secure enough to receive a summons to a new parliament. Writs were sent out naming 16 September as the date. After various delays, it was finally assembled in Westminster in the first week of November 1381.

The purpose of the November parliament was to tie up the legal and administrative ends of the revolt, to hear petitions relating to damages caused by the rebels and to refinance yet again the endless French war. By November 1381, the repercussions of the revolt were still causing acute discord throughout the country. In fact, there was even more tension than had existed at Northampton at the end of the previous year.

At the root of many of these problems was the emerging nature of Richard's kingship. The young king had come of age at Smithfield, giving on that perilous afternoon a glimpse of the selfless bravery for which his father and the best of the Plantagenet dynasty had been famous. But in the aftermath he had shown the dark inclinations of his family's character that lay buried in his breast. He was permanently affected by his encounter with the mob, and the taste of martial law that the days following the revolt afforded him had proven addictive. Through judicial tyrants like Tresilian, Richard prolonged the terror for months after the battles of Mousehold Heath and Billericay. The people had frightened their king, and now the king would frighten his people.

Almost all of the chroniclers remember the months between July and November 1381 as dark, bloody and terrifying. As well as the tit-for-tat executions that had taken place in the Cheap, Englishmen in their hundreds – perhaps in their thousands – were killed by all number of grisly and extraordinarily cruel means. According to the chronicler Adam Usk, the King's commissioners had some rebels dragged to their deaths behind horses, some hanged, some routed with the sword and some dismembered.[1] In many places, the only testimony required to condemn rebels was the accusation of some 'trustworthy' local figure. There was a terrible paranoia sweeping the country, as fear of the King's reprisals against his nobles brought out an equal vindictiveness in his subjects. The Westminster Chronicler wrote of neighbours turning on one another, and of servants accusing their masters of acts of rebellion in order to do them a bloody injustice. A chance misplaced word was enough to condemn a man, as one John Shirley found out: he was executed in Cambridgeshire for having declared in a tavern that he thought John Ball was a true and worthy man.[2] Richard was restoring his royal power not through reform or assertion of the rule of law, but by a barely legal terror in which viciousness had replaced wisdom, and blind fear stalked the troubled land.

If we consider his bitter words to the vanquished rebels at Chelmsford, and then project back from the rest of his troubled reign, it is not hard to imagine that Richard himself was ultimately responsible for the character of the revolt's legal suppression. There seems to have been no check on his youthful instinct to wipe out, rather than to mollify or discipline, his enemies. His first thought in restoring the Crown's dignity was to exercise his own anointed wrath, and though the records are patchy, it is likely that between July and September, anywhere between 1,500 and 7,000 of Richard's subjects died.[3] In many cases they were killed as traitors.

By November, the bloody reprisals (the scale of which would not be seen perhaps until the aftermath of the Monmouth rebellion in 1685, where 3,000 were either killed in battle, executed or transported) had themselves become a threat to the social order of the country. There was a chaotic series of commissions still in action across the country, often with special commissioners operating in the same county and at the same time as senior judges on regular judicial work. The property forfeitures resulting from the deaths and executions were so extensive that an entire new set of escheators (royal officials who dealt with forfeited property) had to be appointed. Malicious litigants had begun to drop accusations of treason and rebellion into ongoing lawsuits, confusing and clogging up the courts. Poor grumblers like John Shirley were meeting with their deaths for mere drunken words, while in counties like Kent the almost tyrannical response of Richard's government was provoking rumours of another wave of rebellion. In short, the country was as unstable as ever, yet it was also decorated with thousands of gibbeted, mutilated and quartered bodies. The bloated and bloodied heads that gazed blindly down from the gates of rebellious towns and cities looked on a country feeling its way not towards harmony but only towards worsening discord.

In addition to this, Richard was still experiencing dire difficulties at the top of government, arising from the personality and politics of his uncle Gaunt, who remained impossible to manage. Despite being absent from the central events of the rebellion (including its suppression), Gaunt found his unpopularity undimmed. And at a time when securing an inexpensive foreign peace to encourage domestic stability should have been the realm's first priority, by late 1381 Gaunt was developing a plan to throw resources into his own ambitious war in Castile.

He was also actively undermining English politics, when once again the moment called for harmony. The revolt had provided him with yet another enemy, this time in the person of Henry Percy. Northumberland's craven refusal to help or harbour the duke at a time when he believed his life was in danger was, to Gaunt, an unforgivable slight. So, since the revolt Gaunt had been doing all he could to humble Percy.

Richard and his council tried on three occasions to pour oil on the troubled waters of his uncle's new feud.[4] They failed. When the two men arrived at Westminster for parliament, they did so with large armed retinues and the real threat of another violent conflict looming (the Londoners, unsurprisingly, stood firmly behind Percy, so there was a strong prospect of yet more rioting against the duke). It took days of formal negotiation, which further delayed the opening of Parliament, to force a rapprochement.

When Parliament did open, it did so in great tension. The consequences of the revolt were obvious merely from the people serving royal office: when the new archbishop-elect William Courtenay, and the new treasurer, Sir Hugh Segrave, made their opening remarks, it would have been hard for all present not to think of their predecessors' ugly fates. Likewise, the presence of Thomas Holland as the new earl of Kent was a reminder of the ruthlessness with which the revolt had been crushed in that county.

But more importantly, there was in November 1381 the first hint that Richard, despite his Smithfield heroics, did not carry with him the faith and trust of the political community. Segrave was forced to take Parliament's debated opinion as to whether the Mile End charters of manumission should be allowed to stand, or were invalid, as the king claimed. In a sign of the commons' divided opinion of Richard's kingship, the official revocation took some considerable effort. First the speaker of Parliament, Sir Richard Waldegrave, attempted to resign his office. Richard refused to accept his resignation, upon which Waldegrave dissembled on behalf of the rest of the commons, saying that they couldn't agree on the matter because (in an improbable excuse) they could not understand what they were being asked. Eventually Richard had to command the new chancellor, Sir Richard le Scrope, to ensure that the repeal went through fully comprehended. After what we can assume was a fair degree of menacing, the king got his way, but his Parliament's reluctance to stand with him against the rebels was a worrying omen.

Even more concerning was the fact that the November parliament went on to demand reform of the royal household. They asked for 'good and worthy people about [the king's] person' and 'that the great company of people on horse and foot who come to the household, be reduced to such a number and comprise such persons that our said lord may live honestly within his own means from now on, without charging his people as has been done before'.

The most telling line in the petition came next: 'Considering also, for the love of God, the grievances and complaints that the poor people have often made about bad governance and outrageous expense, and that they do not know how, and are unable, to secure a remedy'.

Having vacillated over repealing the Mile End charters, the commons were now implying that they thought the recent rebels may have had a point!

Finally the king seems to have accepted that his bloody reprisals were winning him no supporters among the parliamentary commons and the realm at large, for eventually Parliament was allowed to formulate what it considered the best response to the rebellion. Some six months after the revolt had begun it was decided that the only way to bring some form of peace to the country was to issue a national pardon. (It is likely that the new queen, Anne of Bohemia, whom Richard married in January 1382, played a part in convincing her young husband to see sense.) Life could not practically continue for the ordinary people in England with the shadow of death hanging over them indefinitely. As a result, a three-part pardon was issued. Grace was offered to the nobles and gentry – this excused those maverick and technically illegal heroes of the revolt such as Despenser, who might have been guilty of overreaching of their powers during the crisis days of June. Second, grace was offered to the rebels. With the exception of men from the towns of Canterbury, Bury St Edmunds, Beverley, Scarborough, Bridgwater, and Cambridge, those who had been involved in the deaths of Sudbury and Cavendish, and a list of 100 or so named, known miscreants, the rebels were excused their bad behaviour.

Finally a general pardon was issued, offering grace to the ordinary people of England. And in a sense, as 1382 dawned, the great revolt was over.

~

The rebellion of 1381 was in many senses the making of King Richard II. Kings who acceded as minors often found themselves in a difficult position when their time came to grow up. Shaking off the shackles of those men appointed to oversee government in their name usually required some great moment – a statement of manhood; of fitness to rule. Edward III's had come three years into his reign when he overthrew the tyrannical regency of his mother and her lover, Roger Mortimer. More than a century later, the Tudor King Henry VIII marked his coming of age with his first French war. Richard's great moment was Smithfield.

Prior to 1381, Richard was a child. After Smithfield, Richard the man emerged. His wedding and Anne's coronation interrupted the November parliament, which had by that time formally granted the pardon and moved on to arguing about the best way to finance the continuing war – and from that point on, he struggled to free himself and his household from oversight, and to govern entirely as he saw fit.

But Richard's personality and judgement had already been badly warped. He emerged from childhood, and 1381 in particular, with a profound distrust of his subjects and in particular his nobility. He grew up paranoid and vindictive, incensed at any attempts to guide him or to reform his rule. He preferred the company of men like Tresilian and Nicholas Brembre to the higher nobility who ought to have been his natural allies. (Both Tresilian and Brembre were executed on the authority of the so-called Merciless Parliament of 1387, which attempted to purge Richard's household of its most pernicious members.) When his government failed and his nobles and family attempted to coerce him into mending his ways, he raged and thrashed against them. He was a paranoid bully. At his best he was passive-aggressive, and at his worst a tyrant and a brute. During the dark years of 1397–1399 he forced his enemies among the noble classes to seal blank charters, with which he could hold them to any ransom he chose. Just as his great-grandfather Edward II had been considered 'incorrigible' during proceedings leading to his forced abdication, so Richard, when he was deposed in 1399, lost the throne and extinguished the true Plantaganet bloodline forever, having exhausted the patience of his subjects.

Not all of this can be blamed squarely on his experience in 1381. But many of Richard's later problems were to be seen in kernel form during his summer of blood. Part of the reason it spiralled so badly out of control was that when it began Richard had no one around him who could demonstrate the art of governance and of crisis management. This was not a momentary lack of counsel, but a fundamental problem with his reign and with his personality.

Richard's first and greatest misfortune was that he lacked any effective role model for kingship. When he was a child he saw his grandfather, Edward III, at his worst: senile and surrounded by grasping acolytes. His own father did not live long enough to shape Richard in his own mould. In the end, Richard's real role model was his uncle Gaunt, as disastrous a study in rule as he could have had. The boy picked up all of Gaunt's worst faults, without displaying any of his talent. He was a bully, but not authoritative; aggressive in defending the rights of the Crown, but with no true comprehension of its awesome responsibilities; eager to pick and maintain a quarrel, but guileless in making peace.

Likewise, Richard's harsh and divisive personality was there for all to see after the rebellion had been squashed. His vengefulness and his untrustworthiness were what led to the pleas in the November 1381 parliament for an end to the punishments; they were also what turned so many in his realm against him, including – ultimately – his nemesis, cousin, and successor: Gaunt's son, Henry of Derby.

But the story of Richard and Henry, which in many senses began in the Tower, is another story again. In fact, in the winter of 1381/82, as Richard prepared to marry, to become a man and a king, and to put the troublesome revolt behind him, it was a short lifetime away.

∼

If this was Richard's legacy from the revolt, what, then, was England's? The first, baldest truth was that the governing classes acknowledged that a poll tax was foolish and unfair. The November 1381 parliament fudged its way to a new funding of war and national defence that derived from a long-term tax on trade. No direct, regressive attempt at widening the tax base was seen for several generations, and when it was, under Henry VII in 1497, there was another rebellion against the government. The English have always hated poll taxes, and probably always will.

Allied to the hatred of tax was a resentment of the labour laws and their effective imposition of a new form of serfdom, that was legal rather than tenurial in character. While the revolt had little direct effect on labour legislation, fears of serfdom had diminished within a generation. And the labour laws remained as impractical and absurd after the revolt as they had been before it.

But of course the rebellion of 1381 was not just a tax revolt or a revolt against poorly considered labour legislation. It was the first sign that the ordinary people in England were politicised, and could be made angry enough to rise against bad leadership. They cared about foreign policy, and corrupt ministers, and bad laws. And ultimately, they cared about the social compact that Langland characterised in Piers Plowman, when Piers told the knight: 'I shall sweat and strain and sow for us both/And also labour for your love all my lifetime/In exchange for your championship of the Holy Church and me.' There was a profound sense that those high up in society were failing in their godly duties to protect and defend those lower down. Tyler's rebels were really very conservative. Only a few would have believed in Ball's doctrine of total egalitarianism; most simply wanted society and social relations to operate normally again.

And they were not alone. Just as the English rebels had mimicked the *Jacques* who had terrorised the French nobility during the 1350s, so there was an explosion in other lower-class rebellions across Europe during the fifteenth and especially the sixteenth centuries. There were savage uprisings of the agricultural and urban lower orders in Germany, Hungary, Slovenia, Croatia, Finland and Switzerland in the 250 years that followed Tyler's rebellion. All took different forms and involved different local grievances, but all demonstrated that as the medieval period gave way to early modernity the ordinary men (and women) of Europe's kingdoms were beginning by turns to understand, appreciate, resent, defend and vocalise their own place in the social compact. They could communicate complex ideas and move en masse and with abstract purpose. They could appoint and follow leaders in a form that mirrored the political construction of the states and kingdoms they inhabited. And they were prepared to suffer the hideous, vengeful punishments that their insurrection earned them in the name of their righteous cause.

But Tyler's rebellion showed that the English lower orders were among the most advanced in terms of their political development. And so they remained. By the time of Jack Cade's rebellion in 1450 – the next great rising of the English people, led once again from the south-east – the feudal aspects of the great agreement had withered. Serfdom was dead. Cade led an overtly political rebellion, rather than one that demanded the end of lordship or great social reconstitution. His rebels protested policy, not the principles on which society was formed. But even in Cade's context, the compact lived on: the people toiled, and their masters protected them. When it worked, all went well. When it did not, the results were bloody.

Finally, the revolt left us a great story, which was immediately reflected on and retold by some of the great English writers. Chaucer and Gower both wrote about the rebellion – and both paid close attention to the animal instincts of the rebels. From Elizabethan times onwards, the rebellion proved fertile territory for playwrights and historians. John Stow included it in his history, as did other sixteenth-century London chroniclers, and the most popular story was that of one 'John Tyler', usually of Deptford, who brained a sexually lascivious tax-collector to defend the honour of his daughter.

Stow first mentioned the rebellion in 1566, at a time when the fear of popular rebellion would still have reverberated, following Wyatt's rebellion of 1553 against Queen Mary I. Soon the rebellious mob as a terrifying and herdly rabble had become a staple of English literature. Though he never tackled Tyler, Shakespeare dealt with rebellious mobs on numerous occasions. In Henry VI, Part II, Jack Cade was sent up as a pompous ignoramus in a way that would perhaps have amused Thomas Walsingham, when he accuses Lord Say (shortly before cutting off his unfortunate head and sticking it on a pole):

> Thou hast most traitorously corrupted the youth of the realm in erecting a grammar school . . . It will be prov'd to thy face that thou hast men about thee that usually talk of a noun and a verb, and such abominable words as no Christian ear can endure to hear.

Likewise, in what were most likely his additions to the play *Sir Thomas More*, Shakespeare has More remonstrate with a mob protesting the appearance of foreigners who were taking away Englishmen's jobs:

> Grant them removed, and grant that this your noise
> Hath chid down all the majesty of England.
> . . .
> And that you sit as king in your desires,
> Authority quite silenced by your brawl,
> And you in ruff of your opinions clothed :
> What had you got? I'll tell you: you had taught
> How insolence and strong hand should prevail,
> How order should be quelled, and by this pattern
> Not one of you should live an aged man,
> For other ruffians, as their fancies wrought,

209

With selfsame hand, self reasons and self right
Would shark on you, and men like ravenous fishes
Would feed on one another.[5]

This is not far from being an alternative version of another English chancellor's arguments with a rabble: Walsingham's speech for Sudbury as he was dragged to his fate on Tower Hill has a more desperate poignancy but at the core it is the same: the hopeless invocation of reason against the rabble.

It was not long before Tyler's rebellion became more than just grist to the playwrights' mills, and began to be appropriated for political analogy. In 1642 an anonymously written pamphlet called 'The Just Reward of Rebels' used the Kent and Essex rebels' experience as a warning to the Irish rebels of the time; while the most popular eighteenth-century rendition of the story (a chapbook called simply 'The History of Wat Tyler and Jack Strawe') gained popularity around the times of the Jacobite and American revolts against the Hanoverian crown.

In the eighteenth century, Tyler's revolt interested writers including Thomas Paine and Edmund Burke, who used it as material for contemporary arguments about political theory.[6] Later, in the mid-nineteenth century, Friedrich Engels saw in the upheaval of 1848 parallels with Europe's history of medieval class revolt.[7] Even in the twentieth century, Marxist historians gravitated towards the subject of Tyler's rebellion as a rare occasion of life imitating theory.

But perhaps the finest piece of writing about the revolt was by the young Romantic poet Robert Southey, who claimed to be descended from Wat Tyler himself and, as a lusty twenty-something, wrote a play about his supposed ancestor in three frantic nights of work. Like most writers on the revolt, Southey was most fascinated by John Ball, and it is to him that he gave perhaps the best lines in his play (which was published, to Southey's great embarrassment, some two decades after he wrote it, by which time the author had become a hoary old conservative and Poet Laureate).

This epilogue started with the details of John Ball's death; it seems fitting that it ends with Southey's gloriously imagined version of the mad priest's swansong:

> John Ball
> [to Sir John (*sic*) Tresilian]
>
> The truth, which all my life I have divulg'd
> And am now doom'd in torment to expire for,
> Shall still survive – the destin'd hour must come,
> When it shall blaze with sun-surpassing splendour,
> And the dark mists of prejudice and falsehood
> Fade in its strong effulgence. Flattery's incense
> No more shall shadow round the gore-dyed throne;
> That altar of oppression, fed with rites,
> More savage than the Priests of Moloch taught,
> Shall be consumed amid the fire of Justice;
> The ray of truth shall emanate all around,
> And the whole world be lighted!

In the end, the story of the revolt of 1381 – the Peasants' Revolt, or the Great Revolt, or Tyler's Revolt, or whatever else we want to call it – is the story of the relationship between the small men and the great men. The burning injustice that became a mass movement; the small, ungracious serving man who faced down his liege lord, and nearly won; the maverick churchman who preached from the heart instead of from the prayerbook; the fragile victory of a boy wearing the crown of a king; the heroism and the hubris so evident on both sides, likewise the humanity and the cruelty; the fleeting brilliance of a great protest against fundamental wrongs, which may have failed, but inspired the poets five hundred years later: all these sing to us through the centuries, and are what, I think, makes history still worth reading; and worth writing, too.

A revell!

A NOTE ON SOURCES

There are many colourful sources relating to the Peasants' Revolt. The invaluable modern compendium, which brings together a splendid cross-section of them with helpful notes on context, is *The Peasants' Revolt of 1381* by R. B. Dobson (2nd edition, London – most recently reprinted in 2002, though my copy dates from 1983). It remains the best scholarly introduction to the rebellion, its causes and its aftermath. The bibliography is also the best guide to the primary and secondary literature on 1381, although naturally it does not cover a few publications of recent years.

To this we should add the incomplete *Le soulévement des travailleurs d'Angleterre en 1381* by André Réville (Paris, 1898), which first printed many important documents concerning the rebellion. Unfortunately this is hard to obtain outside the large copyright libraries and has never been translated into English. Similarly useful, and similarly hard to find, is Andrew Prescott's meticulous 'The Judicial Records of the Rising of 1381' (University of London PhD thesis, 1984). The hard copy in the British Library was missing at the time of writing, so it can only be consulted on microfilm, or by application to the University of London.

I have consulted numerous other works relating to the revolt – what follows is a selection of the most interesting and useful, arranged roughly in the order that they have been used in this book.

The records of the medieval parliaments have been brilliantly transcribed, translated, arranged and explained in *The Parliament Rolls of Medieval England*, edited by Chris Given-Wilson. I have consulted the electronic version of the rolls, which was released as a single-volume CD-ROM in 2005. It can be purchased at sd-editions.com/PROME/. For an explanation of how labour laws, parliaments and public policy were related, see 'Service, Serfdom and English Labour Legislation, 1350–1500', by Chris Given-Wilson, in *Concepts and Patterns of Service in the Later Middle Ages,* by Anne Curry and Elizabeth Matthew (eds) (Woodbridge, 2000).

The complex politics of London, including John of Gaunt's running feud with the city's merchant oligarchs and the city's rabble, are described in *The Turbulent London of Richard II,* by R. Bird (London, 1949). The case notes regarding the Janus Imperial murder, which I have described here to illustrate the viciousness of London politics and Gaunt's ill-considered use of his executive power to pursue his personal battles, can be found in *Select Cases in the Court of King's Bench*, vol. VII, by G. O. Sayles (ed.). An unpublished article, 'The Murder of Janus Imperial: Law and Politics in London before the Peasants Revolt', by D. G. Jones (2002), explains the case, and can be obtained by direct enquiry via my website: www.summerofblood.com.

The early, rural stages of the revolt are murky. The monastic chroniclers (of whom more below) are all either vague or confused about the revolt's origins. Several articles, however, have been published in an attempt to piece together a coherent narrative of late May and early June 1381. The best is 'The Organization and Achievements of the Peasants of Kent and Essex in 1381', by Nicholas Brooks, published in *Studies in Medieval History presented to R. H. C. Davis*, by H. Mayr-Harting and R. I. Moore (eds) (1985).

For snapshots of the rebellion in Kent, 'The Great Rebellion in Kent of 1381 illustrated from the Public Records' by W. E. Flaherty, in *Archaeologia Cantiana* 3 (1860), is a useful compilation of legal records from Wat Tyler's own county. The Essex equivalent is 'Essex in Insurrection, 1381', by J. A. Sparvel-Bayly, in *Transactions of the Essex Archaeological Society*, NS, 1 (Colchester, 1878). There have been more recent local studies of the south-east but these two allow the reader to engage directly with the legal records made directly after the revolt.

None of the monastic chroniclers are very accurate when dealing with the early stages of the rebellion, but they can be (and have been) usefully cross-referenced to build up a narrative of the revolt in London. The best informed is the so-called 'Anonimalle' chronicler, whose identity is unclear, but who seems to have had the most privileged access to the royal court during the crisis of Corpus Christi weekend. Dobson prints much of the Anonimalle Chronicle in a better translation than appears in *The Great Revolt of 1381*, by Charles Oman (Oxford, 1906 – my copy was published in London, 1989).

The most entertaining of the chronicles is by Thomas Walsingham, the St Albans chronicler. *The St Albans Chronicle: The Chronica Maiora of Thomas Walsingham. Volume I: 1376–1394*, by John Taylor, Wendy R. Childs and Leslie Watkiss (eds and trans.) (Oxford, 2003) is the most recent edition. Walsingham is hysterically biased against the rebels, and he often frames set pieces from the revolt (such as the death of Sudbury and Despenser's victory) as modern parallels to other great events from classical history and the times of the ancient Britons. But he was also an eyewitness to all of the events in St Albans and many of those in London. And his is the best illustration of the moral terror that gripped his class.

Other important chroniclers are the Westminster chronicler and Henry Knighton. The versions I have used are *The Westminster Chronicle 1381–1394*, by L. C. Hector and Barbara F. Harvey (eds) (Oxford, 1982) and *Knighton's Chronicle 1337–1396*, by G. H. Martin (ed.) (Oxford, 1995). Westminster adds useful details on the revolt in London; Knighton is the best source for Despenser's role in subduing the rebellion. Finally, there is Jean Froissart, whose chronicle was most beautifully rendered into English by Lord Berners in *The Chronicles of Froissart*, by G. C. Macaulay (ed.) (London, 1895). Froissart is the most inventive of the chroniclers, but did seem to have good sources at the royal court. I have followed him most notably (and perhaps controversially) in identifying the rebels' envoy to the Tower when they were at Blackheath as Sir John Newton, the keeper of Rochester Castle.

Also useful in understanding events during the London riots is *Memorials of London and London Life 1276–1419*, by H. T. Riley (ed. and trans.) (London, 1868). More recently, so is 'London in the Peasants' Revolt: a portrait Gallery', by A. J. Prescott, from the *London Journal* (1981). *Revolt in London: 11th to 15th June 1381* (London, 1981), by C. M. Barron is another succinct version of the events in London, with additional background on London politics. For incidental material about London, its geography and its traditions, there are many useful sources, to which I have alluded in the footnotes. A couple of volumes can be usefully consulted for an introduction: *Medieval London*, by T. Baker (London, 1970), which provides much useful information about London's architecture. I have also tried to emphasise the importance of the festive mood of Corpus Christi. Readers who wish to learn more should consult 'Corpus Christi and Corpus Regni', by M. Aston in *Past and Present* (1994) and, for more context, *Corpus Christi: The Eucharist in Late Medieval Culture*, by M. Rubin (Cambridge, 1991).

For the rising in Norfolk, *The Rising in East Anglia in 1381*, by E. Powell (Cambridge, 1896), is still very useful. 'The rising of 1381 in Suffolk: its origins and participants', by C. Dyer, in *Proceedings of the Suffolk Institute of Archaeology and History* (1985), should be consulted for information on that county. For Cambridgeshire the *Victoria County History of Cambridgeshire*, vol. III, contains much detail on local politics that is unavailable elsewhere. I have used in this account the character of Bishop Despenser to draw the stories of those counties together in late June 1381. There is a short version of his life in print: *Henry Despenser: The Fighting Bishop*, by Richard Allington-Smith (Dereham, 2003). An important discussion of the letters of John Ball can be found in *Writing and Rebellion: England in 1381*, by Steven Justice (Berkeley, 1994). The best short description of the suppression of the revolt, which revises the idea that the government exercised much restraint in putting down the rebels is A. J. Prescott, '"The Hand of God": the suppression of the Peasants'

Revolt of 1381' in Nigel J. Morgan, (ed.), *Prophecy, apocalypse and the day of doom*: Proceedings of the 2000 Harlaxton Symposium (*Harlaxton Medieval Studies*, 12) (Donnington: Shaun Tyas, 2004).

Other important accounts of the revolt include *Bond Men Made Free*, by R. Hilton (1973), the classic Marxist account of the rising, which sets it in its broader European context, and the six papers presented to the London conference of the Past and Present Society in 1981 collected under the title of *The English Rising of 1381*. For a short history of writing about the revolt, see L. M. Matheson, 'The Peasants' Revolt through Five Centuries of Rumour and Reporting' in *Studies in Philology*, Spring 1992, No. 2. Examples of many of the texts described are to be found in Dobson, *Peasants' Revolt*.

The biographies of Wat Tyler and John Ball in the *Dictionary of National Biography* are good short surveys, although we are always likely to know tantalisingly little about both men. For their betters, including John of Gaunt, the London merchants Walworth, Brembre and Philipot, the earl of Salisbury, Simon Sudbury and so on, there are fuller biographies available in the *DNB*. I have consulted the extremely convenient online version.

NOTES

Foreword

1 Westminster Chronicle.

2 Walsingham.

3 This model of understanding popular rebellion has been best developed by Eric Hobsbawm. For a specific discussion with regards to 1381, the reader should consult Prescott, *Judicial Records*.

4 Leader of the theorists is R. Hilton. See *Bond Men Made Free* for an example of great historical and theoretical rigour but a lack of compelling narrative.

Introduction

1 In *The Nun's Priest's Tale,* Chaucer uses the memory of the revolt as an extended simile for the hullabaloo created when the human and animal characters in that story are chasing a fox.

2 As remembered by the chronicler Henry Knighton.

3 Ibid.

4 A classic account of labour legislation is B. H. Putnam 'The enforcement of the statutes of labourers during the first decade after the Black Death' (1908).

5 As described in the Statute of Labourers, which wrote the Ordinance of Labourers into official law in 1351.

6 This complaint was made at the October parliament of 1377, the first of Richard II's reign.

7 For a scholarly account of the Great Rumour, see R. J. Faith, 'The Great Rumour of 1377 and Peasant Ideology' in *The English Rising of 1381* (Past and Present Society Conference proceedings, 1981). Faith explains the position of rabble-rousers (described in the parliamentary petition of 1377 as 'counsellors, procurers, maintainers, and abettors,' stirring the countryside up with 'counsel ... and manipulation') such as one John Godefray, who appeared before Wiltshire justices, accused of having counselled villeins that 'exemplifications ... by record of the book of ... Domesday' would prove them to be free.

8 Complaint made at the Good Parliament, held April–July 1376. The standard one-volume account is GH Holmes, *The Good Parliament* (Oxford 1975).

9 Description from the chronicle *Vita Ricardi II*, quoted in Dobson, *Peasants' Revolt*.

1 PARLIAMENT

1 Parliament in the fourteenth century was not a place for politicking and party sniping, but a bartering shop between king and political community. Deals were struck in which the Crown traded concessions for reform and better governance for access to the parliamentary commons' grasp of the national wealth in the form of taxation. Between Crown and the commons in Parliament sat the nobility, whose interests tended to side with the Crown. The Crown relied on influential lords in the upper chamber to broker compromise that suited the national interest but also paid for government policy.

2 According to the Parliament Rolls.

3 Ibid.

2 LANCASTER

1 See 'A Note on Sources' for further reading about the Janus Imperial case.

2 The two best biographies of John of Gaunt are S. Armitage-Smith, *John of Gaunt* (repr. London, 1964) and A. Goodman, *John of Gaunt: The Exercise of Princely Power in Fourteenth-Century Europe* (Harlow, 1992).

3 COLLECTIONS

1 Henry Knighton.
2 Ibid.
3 Ibid.
4 Anonimalle Chronicle.
5 Ibid.
6 Ibid.

4 A CALL TO ARMS

1 Anonimalle Chronicle.
2 Anonimalle Chronicle.

5 A GENERAL AND A PROPHET

1 Partly because of Gaunt's notorious obnoxiousness and partly because of his deep regard for the rights of the Crown there was a popular, if mistaken, supposition that the duke of Lancaster coveted the throne for himself.
2 Anonimalle Chronicle.
3 Anonimalle Chronicle.
4 Anonimalle Chronicle – see also H. Eiden, 'Joint action against "bad" lordship: The Peasants' Revolt in Essex and Norfolk', *History*, vol. 83 (1998).
5 Anonimalle Chronicle.

6 BLACKHEATH

1 The Anonimalle Chronicler suggests there were 50,000 on Blackheath Hill and 60,000 in the Essex party north of the Thames. Froissart guessed at 60,000 on the hill.
2 The Anonimalle Chronicle mistakenly places the earls of Buckingham and Suffolk in the Tower with Richard. Buckingham

was either in Wales (as Froissart suggests) or Brittany during the revolt; Suffolk was in East Anglia.

3 We follow Froissart's version of events here: though not always reliable, he did have some decent sources at court, and it seems plausible that the rebels, having seized Newton, would put such a valuable resource to good use.

4 Certainly it stuck in the mind of the Westminster Chronicler, who remembered the 'A revell!' cries.

7 THE TRUE COMMONS

1 For this and more on Corpus Christi, see M. Rubin, *Corpus Christi: The Eucharist in Late Medieval Culture*, (Cambridge, 1991).

2 For a convenient description of Richard's coronation, readers can consult *Richard II*, by N. Saul (Yale, 1997).

3 This idea is explained in G. L. Harriss, *Shaping the Nation* (Oxford, 2005), p. 251.

4 These are the words that Froissart put in Ball's mouth as typifying his stock sermons on the unholy inequality that pervaded in England. They are also filtered through the translation of Berners, which adds to their elegance, even if it detracts from their authenticity.

8 THE BRIDGE

1 Gower, *Vox Clamantis*.

2 For a discussion of accusations levelled at aldermen connected with Walworth in the aftermath of the revolt, see Bird, *Turbulent London*.

3 Anonimalle Chronicle.

4 Ibid.

9 FIRST FLAMES

1 For details of the history and architecture of the Temple, see Baker, *Medieval London*.

2 For timing see Westminster Chronicle.

10 UNDER SIEGE

1 Prescott, 'Portrait Gallery'.

2 For more neat examples of the private feuds that played out during the rebels' time in London, see Prescott, 'Portrait Gallery'.

3 Anonimalle Chronicle.

4 Ibid.

11 WAR COUNCIL

1 Walsingham.

2 Froissart.

12 MILE END

1 London inquisition before the sheriffs of 20 November 1382, reprinted in Dobson, *Peasants' Revolt* and Oman, *Great Revolt*. We must, however, bear in mind that politics lie behind much of what is recorded in the sheriffs' inquisition. There is a chance that Farringdon is erroneously placed here.

2 Flaherty, 'Great Rebellion in Kent' records that Thomas Noke of the Hundred of Tenham was accused after the revolt of killing James French at Mile End.

3 Only the Anonimalle Chronicle places Tyler at Mile End. While the Anonimalle's author seems largely reliable with his description of events in London, on this occasion there is cause for doubt. The totally different character between the demands made at Mile End and the following day at Smithfield seem to bear out the supposition drawn from the rest of the chronicles, i.e. that Tyler was absent from this meeting, and probably closer to the wilder, more militant group of rebels that surrounded the Tower.

4 Anonimalle Chronicle.

13 THE TOWER

1 Several of the chroniclers record that Sudbury said Mass that morning. The medieval Mass was strikingly dissimilar to anything experienced in the mainstream Catholic Church since the Second Vatican Council of the 1960s. For a brief glimpse of the Tridentine

Mass – a reasonable approximation of the high medieval ceremony – recreated in a modern setting, see *nytimes.com/packages/html/us/20071104_LATINMASS_FEATURE/index.html* and *liturgy.dk/default.asp? Action=Details&Item=559*, for a Scandinavian interpretation.

2 M. Aston, 'Corpus Christi and Corpus Regni', in *Past and Present* (1994).

3 Walsingham.

4 Ormrod, 'The Peasants' Revolt and the Government of England', *Journal of British Studies*, 29 (1990) adds physical evidence to Walsingham's lurid account of the sack of the Tower.

5 According to Walsingham.

6 Although by this point in his account it is almost certain that Walsingham's account of Sudbury's death is more hagiography than hard, historical fact – the sentiments of Sudbury's supposed argument ring true. One suspects, however, that Walsingham's portrayal of Sudbury's Christ-like compassion for his executors may be a step too far.

14 THE RUSTICS RAMPANT

1 Froissart records the 'great venom' of those who stayed behind in London, with the intention to slay and rob the folk of the City. Read as a whole, the chroniclers seem to infer a greater malice in the rebels who remained in London after the departure of eastern rebels following Mile End.

2 The chroniclers differ on the number of executions that took place on Tower Hill. The Anonimalle Chronicler claims that Sudbury, Hales and Appleton were killed there, shortly followed by John Legge and 'a certain juror', and that these were the heads carried to Westminster, while three others executed around the City, presumably about midday, were added to the grisly display once the procession returned to London Bridge. The monk of Westminster agrees that five were killed on Tower Hill, but implies that all five were killed together. Walsingham and Froissart record that Legge was killed with Sudbury, Hales and Appleton (but do

not mention the juror); Knighton, in a muddled account, records seven Tower Hill executions.

3 See City of London Letter Book H, in Dobson, *Peasants' Revolt*. Stepney was, in 1381, known as Stebenhithe.

4 For Richard's particular love of Westminster Abbey, see Stanley, *Westminster Abbey*.

5 London Letter Book H.

6 Honeybourne, *Sketch Map of London*.

7 Prescott, 'Portrait Gallery'.

8 Ibid.

9 Ibid.

10 Dobson, *Peasants' Revolt*.

11 Barron, *London in the Later Middle Ages*.

12 Ibid.

13 J. Stow, *Survey of London* (1598).

14 Ibid.

15 CRISIS

1 Timings for Saturday, 15 June derive from the Anonimalle Chronicle, rather than the Westminster Chronicle. The latter puts the time of Richard's visit to Westminster much earlier in the day. But the Anonimalle Chronicle and City of London Letter Book H both agree that disorder continued until late on Saturday afternoon. The Anonimalle Chronicle times the King's visit to Westminster at 3 p.m., whereas Letter Book H records discord in the City until vespers (around 6 p.m.). 5 p.m. therefore seems a reasonable estimate for the time of the Smithfield conference.

2 Anonimalle Chronicle.

3 A.J. Prescott, *Digitising the Event* (freemasonry.dept.shef.ac. uk, 2005) reports that Robert Bennett of Barford St John, a convicted felon and government approver, executed on the evidence of a Middlesex jury for allegedly taking part in the burning of the Savoy and Clerkenwell Priory, claimed that Imworth's wife had entrusted him with six silver spoons as the rebels approached.

4 For a history of the abbey, and much of the below, see Stanley, *Westminster Abbey*.

5 Timing according to the Anonimalle Chronicle.

6 Stanley, *Westminster Abbey*.

16 SMITHFIELD

1 The most famous early description of Smithfield comes from William Fitzstephen in his 'Description of London', *c.* 1170.

2 Levelling charges of treason against rebels in the aftermath of the revolt was certainly made easier if the authorities could paint them as having organised militarily beneath flags and pennons, but given their obvious deference to Wat Tyler as leader, entrusted to negotiate on behalf of them all, it is reasonable not to doubt the chroniclers' assertions that 'the commons arrayed themselves in bands of great size' (Anonimalle Chronicle).

3 For a brief description of St Bartholomew's see Baker, *Medieval London*.

4 Walsingham records that it was Sir John Newton, the rebels' one-time captive and Keeper of Rochester Castle, who was sent to summon Tyler. It would have made for a logical choice, but in the account of Smithfield we are obliged to follow the Anonimalle Chronicle in light of its greater overall accuracy, attention to circumstantial detail, and probable eyewitness status.

5 In the outlaw legends, which were probably beginning to gain mainstream oral popularity late in the fourteenth century, a respectful meeting between the outlaws and the king was a standard denouement. See S. Knight and T. Ohlgren, *Robin Hood and Other Outlaw Tales* (Kalamazoo, 1997) for a collection of outlaw stories.

6 Anonimalle Chronicle.

17 SHOWDOWN

1 Walsingham.

2 According to the Anonimalle Chronicle. Other sources have Tyler dead at the time of the initial scuffle in front of Richard II.

18 RETRIBUTION

1 The commission is printed in Dobson, *Peasants' Revolt*.
2 The narrative that follows relies on the first-hand witness account by Thomas Walsingham.

19 THE BISHOP

1 We can assume Ball's movements based on his appearance in Coventry in mid-July.
2 Walsingham and Knighton collected examples of Ball's letters – examples from the two chroniclers are printed in Dobson, *Peasants' Revolt*.
3 Knighton records the fullest account of Despenser's progress through East Anglia.
4 Froissart gives a romantic, and perhaps faintly ludicrous, account of Salle's death at the hands of a mob.

20 COUNTER-TERROR

1 Westminster Chronicle.
2 Recorded in Walsingham.
3 Knighton.
4 The Parliament Rolls from the parliament of November 1381 give a lengthy account of the unrest in Cambridge on Corpus Christi weekend.

21 NORWICH

1 See Eiden, 'Joint action'.
2 Cf footnote 1, Chapter Nineteen, above.
3 See Prescott, 'Judicial Records'.

22 VENGEANCE

1 See Prescott, '"The Hand of God": the Suppression of the Peasants' Revolt of 1381'.
2 Prescott, 'Judicial Records'.
3 Walsingham, who recorded the battle, presented it as a modern parallel to Boudicca's last stand.

4 Walsingham.
5 Ibid. Walsingham ascends to new peaks of glee when he describes Richard's pompous denunciation of the rebels.

Epilogue

1 Quoted in Prescott, "'Hand of God'".
2 Ibid.
3 The first figure is Prescott's minimum estimate for the number of rebels killed in battle and by order of the royal commissioners and justices (see Prescott, "'Hand of God'"); the second is the number recorded by the Monk of Evesham, a chronicler who wrote a life of Richard.
4 Details on Richard's attempts to quell the dispute can be found in K. Towson, "'Hearts warped by passion": The Percy-Gaunt dispute of 1381', in *Fourteenth Century England III*, ed. W. M. Ormrod (Woodbridge, 2004).
5 My thanks to Oliver Morgan for his thoughts on Shakespearean rabbles, and for pointing out the two passages quoted.
6 For all the above examples, see L. M. Matheson, 'The Peasants' Revolt through Five Centuries of Rumor and Reporting' in *Studies in Philology*, Spring 1992, No. 2.
7 E. Burke, *Appeal from the New to the Old Whigs*; T. Paine, *Rights of Man: Part Two*; F. Engels, *The Peasant War in Germany*.

INDEX

205; St Albans, acts to defend 165, 166; Sudbury and 78–9, 102, 116; in Tower of London 70–1, 75, 78–9, 101–3, 108–10, 111; 'traitors', sanctions rebels taking of 116, 120–1, 123–4, 125–6, 127; vindictiveness 162, 176, 177, 190, 191, 192, 196, 197, 200–1, 202, 204, 205–6; Walworth counsels attacking reaction to rebellion 108–10, 111, 137–9, 152–5

Rikeden, Robert 58

Rochester Castle, Rochester 59–60, 61, 62, 65, 72

Rotherhithe, Surrey 80, 82–4, 101, 113, 118

Royal Wardrobe 127–8, 143

Salisbury, earl of *see* Montagu, earl of Salisbury, William

Salle, Sir Robert 167, 173, 185

Savoy Palace, London 1, 2, 8, 34, 35, 89, 90, 91, 93, 94–6, 97, 98, 99, 101, 125, 189

Scales, Sir Roger 184, 185

Schep, John 168

Scotland 14, 22, 26, 27, 28, 35, 36, 37, 57, 189

Scrope, Sir Richard le 203

Segrave, Sir Hugh 38, 166, 203

Segynton, Robert de 58

Septvantz, William 62, 65

serfdom 11, 16, 81–2, 115, 147, 193, 207, 208

serjeants-at-arms 44, 84

Sewale, Sir John 45, 46, 51, 58, 62

Shakespeare, William 209–10

Shirley, John 201, 202

Sir Thomas More (Shakespeare) 209–10

Sittingbourne, Kent 62

Skeet, Thomas 187, 188

Smithfield, London 100, 138, 139, 141–7, 149–54, 159, 160, 162, 168, 170, 176, 190, 200, 203, 205

Somenour, Richard 127, 134

Somerset 3, 191

South-East of England: army in 20, 57; low morale within 20; population in, 1380 43; rebellion spreads throughout 136, 138, 160, 162–6, 171; tradition of rebellion within 208 *see also under individual county, town and village*

Southey, Robert 199, 210, 211

Southwark, Surrey 1, 55, 72, 74, 78, 85–90, 108, 118, 133, 144

Spicer, Clement 58

St Albans, Hertfordshire 105–7, 160, 162–6, 172, 199, 200

St Andrew's Priory, Northampton 25, 27

St Bartholomew's Hospital, London 139, 144, 151, 154

St James Garlickhithe church, London 130, 131

St Magnus church, London 86, 88

St Martin-in-the-Vintry church, London 130

St Martin-le-Grand church, London 97, 98

St Mary Arches church, London 162–3

St Paul's Cathedral, London 34, 89, 128

Standish, Sir Ralph 151

Starr, Marjery 180

Statute of Labourers, 1349 14–16, 21

Statute of Winchester, 1285 147

Steeple Morden, Cambridgeshire 181

Stow, John 208–9

the Strand, London 35, 89, 93, 96

Straw, Jack 8, 73, 82, 85, 86, 105, 107, 119, 125, 162, 200

Sudbury, archbishop of Canterbury, chancellor, Simon 60; death 121–4, 126–7, 134, 154, 164, 171, 199, 204, 210; John Ball and 61, 118–19; parliament, Northampton, 1380 27, 28, 29, 30; rebels target 64, 74–5, 79, 83, 84, 108, 116, 117–19, 121–4, 126–7; resigns chancellorship 78–9; Richard's permission to seek out 'traitors' condemns 116, 117–19, 121–4, 126–7; Rotherhithe 83, 84, 101

Suffolk 50, 113, 136, 167, 177, 183, 186, 190, 192–3

Sussex 3, 161

Sybil, Walter 86

taxation: of clergy 31–2; Essex, reaction within to poll tax, 1380 43–7; evasion of 22, 43, 45–7; of middle orders 19, 29; parliament and 19, 21, 22; poll tax, 1377 21, 22; poll tax, 1378 2, 30; poll tax, 1379 2, 22, 30, 31–2, 54; poll tax, 1380 2, 30–1, 32, 40, 42–7; poll tax 1990 3; tax-collecting commissions 32, 42–7, 49, 51, 57, 64, 84, 119, 197; on trade 22, 26, 28, 207

LIST OF ILLUSTRATIONS

The author and publisher are grateful to the following for permission to reproduce their copyright material. While every effort has been made to trace the owners of copyright material reproduced herein, the publishers would like to apologise for any omissions and will be pleased to incorporate missing acknowledgements in any future editions.

William Blake's nineteenth-century impression of the pilgrim road to Canterbury. *(Private Collection/The Bridgeman Art Library)*

John of Gaunt, Duke of Lancaster. (Private Collection/The Bridgeman Art Library)

A romanticised image of William Walworth, Mayor of London. *(© National Portrait Gallery, London)*

Lesnes Abbey. *(© Michael Jenner/Alamy)*

King Richard II, last of the Plantagents. *(Private Collection/The Stapleton Collection/The Bridgeman Art Library)*

John Ball leads the rebels against the government. *(© British Library Board. All Rights Reserved/The Bridgeman Art Library)*

The King meets his subjects. *(© Mary Evans Picture Library)*

The Savoy Palace. *(© Getty Images)*

The destruction of the Savoy Palace. *(© Popperfoto/Getty Images)*

Sudbury and Hales are killed. *(© akg-images/British Library)*

Wat Tyler attackes a poll tax collector. *(© Mary Evans Picture Library)*

The showdown at Smithfield. *(© Time & Life Pictures/Getty Images)*

A nineteenth-century version of Tyler's death. *(Private Collection/ The Bridgeman Art Library)*

King Henry IV. *(© Philip Mould Ltd, London/The Bridgeman Art Library)*

Jack Cade's rebellion, 1450. *(Private Collection/The Bridgeman Art Library)*

Walworth's dagger. *(Fishmongers' Hall, London, UK/The Bridgeman Art Library)*

John Gower. *(© Mary Evans Picture Library)*